CHILDHOOD LOST

Linda A. Goodlin

ISBN: 978-1-61244-749-0
Library of Congress Control Number: 2019906252

Printed in the United States of America

Halo Publishing International
1100 NW Loop 410
Suite 700 - 176
San Antonio, Texas 78213
www.halopublishing.com
contact@halopublishing.com

ACKNOWLEDGEMENTS

I first want to thank God for giving me the desire to write in the Christian genre for His glory. I would never have become an author if it hadn't been for His hand in my life.

To my dear husband Tom. This year marks fifty one years together: Thank you for helping me to grow into the woman that I am. You've always pushed me just the right amount to be the best that I can be. You are the wind beneath my wings.

To my three children; Amy Lynn Goodlin King, Tom Goodlin, Jr., and David Goodlin, AND my four grandchildren; Casey King, Brady King, Laryssa Goodlin and Katrina Goodlin. You've all been such an inspiration to me, in your actions, and by each of you being the unique individuals that you are. I love you all so very much, and I want to share my stories and my memories with you so that "Grandma" will live on in your hearts forever.

To my great-nephew Torrey Wigfield: Thank you for lending me your handsome, thought-filled face for the cover of this book. Torrey I've watched you grow into an awesome young man. I'm so proud of your acting and singing abilities, and of the gentle-man you are. You're a gift from God to all who know and love you.

To all of my friends, family, and book club ladies who have read my first novel, and requested that I do a follow up to "From Across the Pond." Thank you for your support, kind words, cards, and letters. I've truly been blessed with many wonderful new friends, publishers, and editors who continue to inspire me to keep on telling the stories of the coal miners and their families.

CONTENTS

CHILDHOOD LOST
PART ONE

CHAPTER ONE

WILLIAM MILLWARD

Tuesday – March 31, 1891 – Winds of Change

"Hey, William! Ya comin' to the union meetin' tonight?" Peter O'Malley called out as he jogged to catch up with me, his friend and co-worker.

"No, I don't think I'll be comin' to that meetin'. Anna's close to givin' birth again and I want to stay around the house as much as I can when I'm not workin," I replied.

It wasn't like me to lie to anyone, but the truth was I just didn't want any part of the strike that was to come. There were rumors going around that H.C. Frick was getting fed up with all the talk of strikes, and the coal police were joined by the Pinkerton Agency to stop any more trouble that striking miners could cause.

Times were getting worse for the miners. Frick no longer wanted to give company-owned housing, saying he wasn't in the housing business. Many miners were given the choice to either buy the home they lived in or move out. Many men were complaining about the working conditions and unsafe practices that they were forced into. With the price of coal going down, they were instructed to rob the beams that held up the roof of the mine, causing weak areas and mines to cave in.

"I'm sorry to hear that you won't be comin' with us, William. We miners have to stick together to get changes made. If we don't, Frick won't budge in givin' us anything. I hope you'll change your mind and join your co-workers in the fight for justice. You know how the men feel about scabs that cross the picket lines!" Peter shouted as he turned to go to his home in Central.

I shook my head and continued to walk towards Rocktown Road where Anna and I lived with our five children. The house was getting very crowded with such a large family. We had been discussing moving to a small farm two miles away in Frye Hollow. I'd have to walk farther to work but it would be a good move for our family.

With all the trouble among the workers at the mine, I felt it was time to leave our little house that was owned by the mine. I also wanted to stop dealing with the company store that took most of my pay each week. The men who wanted to strike were also disputing the unfair practices of the company store. The coal company was the only one making a profit by forcing the workers to buy everything on script at the company store and not giving actual money for an honest day's work. No miner could ever purchase anything from the surrounding towns because they didn't have cash. If the miners even tried to buy from another merchant, they were boycotted by the company and then couldn't get credit at the company store until the mine owner gave them permission, which could take months.

As I walked the rest of the way home, I thought about the past eleven years. I'd come to America from Wales in 1880 when the mines there were goin' under. When I came here I was making a good living while working for the Maurice Painter Coal Company, which founded Central Mine and Coke Works. I was a boarder at a large house that was owned by a family from Poland. In order to save as much money as I could for the first two years I'd been in America, I slept on a small cot in a large upstairs room with several other miners. My savings helped to bring my brother Joseph and his wife Anna to America.

At first, the Maurice Painter Coal Company had been productive. Mr. Painter was a fair, hard-working man. He and his son lived in a brick, two-story, company-owned house on First Street in the little village of Central, Pennsylvania. His housekeeper, Gretchen Klink, lived next door in a two-story house that had originally been rented to her brother, Hans, who had been the mine foreman. When Hans was killed in a mine explosion, Mr. Painter made an arrangement with Gretchen for her to continue living in the house and to care for his son, Jacob. The explosion that had killed Hans also took the life of Joseph Millward, my brother. Anna was with child at the time of Joseph's death.

Anna had been very upset when I proposed marriage to her on the same day as the death of her young husband, but she soon realized the cruelty of life in a coal patch town. With no means of paying the rent, and no money for passage back to Wales, Anna agreed to marry me.

The small house Joseph and Anna had been renting had only four rooms: a kitchen, a small living room, and two bedrooms. There was an outhouse in the backyard and a small, covered back porch attached to the kitchen. When the young couple first saw their little house they had been full of enthusiasm, but now that Joseph was gone Anna couldn't imagine having another man live with her.

To save Anna from embarrassment and gossip, I enclosed the porch to make a small room, where I slept. The room was only large enough for a small bunk with a few nails on the wall to hang up my clothes, but I had been determined to be a gentleman to Anna. I even offered to pay her passage back to Wales in the coming spring, after her baby was born.

Although I had suggested a marriage of convenience, it wasn't long before I began having feelings for Anna. Not only was she gentle and beautiful, she was also a good and faithful woman. Each day that her body blossomed with my brother's child inside of her, I saw a sadness in her eyes that I wished I could wipe away. The winter of 1881-1882 was very hard on both of us. I worked twelve-hour days, only to return home to sleep in my cold little room alone. The brick chimney where the coal stove stood in the kitchen was all that kept me from freezing that first winter. I'd built a tiny bunk along that inside wall of the porch for a good reason. Shortly after our marriage, I was surprised to come home from the mine one evening to find that Anna had braided a small rug and had put a woolen quilt on my bunk. I knew that it was Anna and Joseph's wedding quilt by the wedding-ring pattern of the quilt patches. This made me both happy and sad at the same time. I do cherish Anna's kindness.

Anna had to quickly learn the ways of life in this strange coal patch town. It didn't take her long to befriend several of the other immigrant women. Colleen O'Malley and Gretchen Klink became her best friends. Besides keeping house for Mr. Painter, Gretchen was the town midwife. Colleen was a wonderful cook and gardener. She came often to visit with Anna, and to pray with her.

The first year was hard indeed. When little James was born, Anna began to trust in me more. Soon she was looking at me with the same fondness I had been feeling for her. It was no longer a marriage of convenience, but a commitment to the child that Joseph had fathered and I willingly and lovingly wanted to raise as my own.

The love between us grew. Although this baby was actually my nephew, I felt the love of being a father to the child. Ten months later, Anna gave birth to a little brother for James, and we named him Benjamin. Then Sarah was born in 1884 and Jacob in 1886.

There were many changes within the mine and the coke works, but I continued to work as much as I could to support our growing family. Anna gave birth to Delilah in 1888.

There was discontent among the workers. Unfortunately the coke business was suffering a depression at the time.

I felt a chill go up my spine just thinking about all of the changes going on. As I got closer to home, I could hear the chatter of little voices and could smell homemade bread.

"Where are my little angels?" I shouted as I came into the kitchen.

"Papa, Papa, Papa," a chorus of voices sang out.

"Hello, my love! Have ya had a hard day?" Anna said as she planted a kiss upon my cheek.

"Aye, we'll talk of it later. Tell me now what this brood has put you through all the day," I said.

"James and Benjamin have gone fishin'. I thought they'd be back home by now. Sarah, Delilah, and Jacob are playin' so I can get supper on the table. I've hot water on the stove for you to wash. Would you call the boys in from the creek?" Anna replied.

I went out to the back yard to holler for the boys, but saw that they were coming through the back field. Neither one had a line of fish. In fact, both of my oldest children had long faces as they approached.

"No luck fishin' today?" I asked.

"Naw. We left our favorite fishin' hole when Patrick O'Malley tried to pick a fight," James replied.

"What? Patrick's been your best friend. Why'd he want to go and pick a fight with ya?" I asked.

"He said his pa called ya a damn scab, and said that ya never want to stick up for the miners' rights. What's a damn scab, Pa?" Benjamin asked.

"Benjamin, shut up. You weren't supposed to tell Pa 'bout it." James shouted.

"All right boys, let's get washed up and go in and eat supper, then we'll talk about this later before you go to bed. Don't mention this in front of your mum. No sense in worryin' her, now is there?" I whispered.

Anna came out onto the porch and poured hot water into a large galvanized washtub that was kept on a small table. I washed as much of the coal dust from my hair and body as possible before comin' into the clean kitchen. Towels and a clean shirt hung on the nails above the shelf in what we used as a makeshift bathroom. This was the room that I had used as a bedroom when we were first married.

Getting all five children settled took quite some time. Anna put all of the children's plates in front of them and then settled into her own chair. I talked with each child about their day. James, Benjamin, and Sarah attended school a half-mile away on Snyder Town Road. The boys didn't like goin' to school, but Sarah loved book learnin' and she didn't hesitate to tell her brothers how silly they were for not likin' school.

Delilah jabbered about the ragdoll that Anna had made for her out of scraps.

After all of the children had eaten, the oldest three cleared the table. Anna was teaching our children at an early age to help with the chores. Sarah seemed to take pride in telling her brothers what to do in the kitchen.

"James, I'll finish up the dishes if you'll wash the little ones for Mum," Sarah said.

"I'd like to spend some time with James and Benjamin if ya don't mind, Sarah. I'll be sure that James does his share of cleaning," I said.

"That sounds good. I'll get the little ones ready for bed. Don't be too long. I know you're tired. Your eyes have worry lines around 'em," Anna said.

Once we were out of earshot of Anna, I turned to the boys. "So, tell me what was said today that got you both so riled up," I asked.

"Patrick called ya a damn scab!" Benjamin cried.

"Now, Benjamin, ya know ya aren't to curse. Don't let me ever hear ya sayin' *damn* again. Ya want to know what a scab is? That's what they call a man who crosses the picket line when there's a strike goin' on," I said.

"What's a strike, Pa?" James asked.

"Well, boys, the men at the mine aren't very happy with their pay or their workin' conditions. A strike is when the men get together and stop diggin' the coal. They stop workin' and they go to all the other coal mines and try to get all of the other miners to stop workin', too. If a man wants to mind his business and just keep on a-workin' when everyone else wants to strike, they call him a scab. It isn't a very nice name and it's not a good situation to find yourself in. Strikes can become violent real fast and people can get hurt. Now, you just pay no mind to Patrick and don't be fightin' with him 'bout this. Your pa's no scab, but I also don't want to be part of a strike. Let me handle this problem in my own way. Ya just keep on bein' friends at school. Ya hear me?" I asked.

"Yes, Pa. We won't do no fightin'," James and Benjamin answered quietly.

We all went inside without saying another word. I was glad that the children didn't know how bad the situation really was. Tomorrow would not be a good day for the miners of southwestern Pennsylvania. I could feel it in my bones. A storm was a-brewin'.

Once all of the children were put down to bed, me and Anna turned out all of the kerosene lanterns and went to our bedroom. Anna rolled her pillow in half and placed it behind her knees.

"Ya be hurtin' tonight, love?" I asked.

"The babe seems to be pressin' on my spine tonight. The only way I'm comfortable is if I sleep flat on my back with my legs propped up," Anna replied.

"Ya sure are a pretty sight, lyin' there in the moonlight with your hair all 'round your face, like an angel," I whispered.

"Oh, ya be full of useless compliments! I'm big as a cow and just as slow, too. Why, I can't even keep up with the little ones when they decide to run about the yard," Anna laughed.

"Anna, I love ya dearly, and I'm sorry I can't make a better life for ya, but if we move to Frye Hollow after the babe's born, we'll have more room there in the farmhouse. We'll even be able to sell some vegetables from the garden for cash," I said.

"It's a big decision, William. We do need more space for our growin' family. I just worry how we'll pay for a house," Anna replied.

"My cousin says the old Trout Homestead is just sittin' empty. No one lives there, and since they're distant cousins of ours we can use the place as we see fit. Johnny Trout says he has all he can handle with the small house and barn to care for. He says we can live there as long as we want to. 'Course we'll have to do our share, raisin' a cow and maybe a few pigs. The farmers all help each other at butcherin' time and the womenfolk work in the garden and process the food together, too. It could be a good thing for ya. There are several families already settled in Frye Hollow. Many people are gettin' out of the company-owned houses. It's time we do, too," I exclaimed.

"Do you really think it would be best, William?" Anna asked.

"Yes, I do. Especially now that the men are talkin' of goin' out on strike and everyone is in an uproar. We'd be better off if we didn't owe the coal company anythin'," I replied.

"William, are ya in any danger?" Anna whispered.

"I do my job and keep to myself, Anna. I don't want trouble with anyone, and I don't want my wife to be a-frettin'," I said as I leaned towards Anna to plant a kiss on her cheek.

"Sleep well, William. I'll try not to worry, but we've seen what a strike can do," Anna replied.

"Nothin' we can do 'bout it tonight. Let's get some sleep, and tomorrow evenin' we'll make plans to take the children to Frye Hollow. If you're feelin' well, maybe we can have a picnic on Sunday after church," I said.

"Oh, that would be wonderful," Anna said.

I didn't want to upset Anna, but I knew there were bad times ahead. Many of the miners were striking, and I'd heard about the march set to take place this very night in Mount Pleasant. Although I wanted no part of it, I would be affected just like every miner would be. The working relationships and friendships we'd forged when we'd first come to America were going to be tested.

The companies had only one thing in mind: profitability. If they weren't making a profit, they could pull out of the small mines and do business with the larger companies.

Little Nipper

CHAPTER TWO

JAMES D. MILLWARD

Thursday – April 2, 1891 – End of School Days

I'll never forget the way my pa talked to me and Benjamin two nights ago when he got home from the mine. It's like he knew somethin' bad was about to happen but he just couldn't tell us what it was. Pa had never talked to us like we were men instead of just little boys of eight and nine years old. Before that night in March, we didn't know or understand what it truly meant to be a coal miner.

As Benjamin and I walked to school the next day, I wished we could stay at home with Ma and the little ones. When we entered the schoolhouse, Miss Hodgekiss, our teacher, was sitting at her desk with her head bent, like she was prayin' or somethin'.

We all liked Miss Hodgekiss. She was a tiny woman with dark hair and a bright smile. She came to school each day on a big brown horse. Patrick said he once saw her jump a fence up near the Funk Farm, where she lived. Don't know if I believe that, but she sure does sit that horse as well as any man I've seen ridin'.

"Children, come in and be seated. Quiet, please!" Miss Hodgekiss sternly said.

"She sure looks mad 'bout somethin'," Benjamin whispered.

"I said to be quiet! That means no talking or whispering!"

I knew right on that it wasn't goin' to be a good day. Miss Hodgekiss was always nice, never gettin' upset when we'd come inside, but today was different. Most all of us kids knew to sit down and mind our manners.

"I'd like you all to take out your slates and—"

Before Miss Hodgekiss could finish her sentence, my pa came into the classroom.

"Miss Hodgekiss, I'm takin' James out of school today. He won't be returnin'. Come with me, James," Pa said as he quickly turned to leave without so much as givin' Miss Hodgekiss any explanation.

I was really afraid of what had happened to make my pa be so short with my teacher.

"Pa, what's wrong?" I cried.

"Somethin' bad has happened and I need you to come to work in the mine with me," Pa answered. Then he began to run towards the mine, with me following as quickly as I could behind him.

When we got to the mine superintendent's office, a crowd was gathered around the entrance. There were several coal police and some official-looking men in suits with badges that said *Pinkerton Agency* on them. All of the miners were standin' together near Mr. McClure, the new mine owner.

"Ya stand beside me, listen, and keep quiet. Ya understand, boy?" Pa whispered.

"Yes, sir!" I didn't realize how badly I was shakin' until I finally caught my breath. Lookin' around I saw I wasn't the only boy standin' there, although I may have been one of the youngest.

"Quiet down, everyone!" Mr. McClure shouted.

Once the crowd was under control, Mr. McClure stood up on an empty wooden box so he could be seen by everyone who was gathered there.

"We're a-wastin' time, so listen up. There's been trouble at the Morewood Mine. A large group of miners wrote up a list of demands. They're askin' to weigh the coal at the tipples. They want an eight-hour work day, extra pay for workin' in a wet place or for narrow workin' space. They want a ten-percent raise, a limit on house rent, and a mandatory three-day notice for strikes, lockouts, quitting, or firing a man. They also said that they want only union men working.

Now, you've all read the notice put up on March 25, 1891 by H.C. Frick Coke Company and McClure Coke Company with a sliding scale of wages, in which wages would be determined by the selling price of coke, based on a $1.75-per-ton minimum. This scale, which is to last for three years, gives the men a nine-hour work day, and precludes the possibility of striking, is to be signed on an individual basis by each man who wants to work," Mr. McClure exclaimed.

"That's an insult! The company is trying to trick us by posting the scale late at night, as if it was approved by labor leaders. You're givin' us nothin'," Peter O'Malley shouted.

"Shut up, O'Malley! You were at the Morewood Mine last night, so get off the premises, and don't come back to work," Mr. McClure replied.

"You can't do that to me. I've been a good worker," Peter O'Malley yelled.

"Not only can I fire you, I'll have your family put out of your house as well!" Mr. McClure shouted as he turned to the coal police and gave them directions to the O'Malley home.

"Pa, can Mr. McClure do that?" I was so confused by all that I was hearing, yet this I did understand: If you didn't go along with the mining company you would lose not only your job but your house, too.

"Yes, James, the coal companies can do whatever they want. That's why the men want to strike and join the United Mine Workers union. I'll explain more to you later when we get home tonight, but for now just keep quiet and do as I say," Pa whispered.

I watched as Mr. O'Malley ran towards his house with the coal police close behind him. I began to shake with fear. What if we got evicted from our little house? Pa didn't need to tell me to keep quiet at this point, because I was speechless.

"If anyone else has a mind to join the union, go on now and don't come back. Those of you who want to work, get on in the mine. Time's a-wastin'," Mr. McClure shouted.

"Millward, come here! Do you want your boy to start workin' with you?" Mr. McClure asked.

"Yes, sir," Pa replied.

"All right then, go to the company store and get him equipped. I'll pay sixty-five cents a day, and I'll add it to your script. Hurry along, and make sure he knows the rules. I'll start him as a nipper, opening and closing the section doors for the mule drivers," Mr. McClure said as he turned to go to the mine office.

We'd walked almost the whole way to the company store before I got the nerve to talk to Pa.

"Pa, how far down in the mine do I have to go?" I asked.

"The first door is about a mile down. I'll take you there and show you what to do. It's the easiest job in the mine. You'll do just fine," Pa replied.

At the company store, Pa asked the clerk for a small mining hat with a lantern on the front of it. He also got me work boots, a coat, and work gloves. Being that I'd be working the doors, I wasn't in need of a pickaxe or shovel.

I watched as the clerk took out a ledger book and wrote down all of the items we got. All these supplies would all come out of my pa's pay. Now I began to understand why we never had much to live on. Everything my family got at the company store was put into that ledger.

Pa helped me put on the work boots and then we practically ran the whole way back to the mine. Before we went into the mine office, Pa said, "Let me do the talkin', boy. As of today, you're twelve years old. Don't tell anyone any different, even when you're not at work."

"But, Pa, that's a lie! Ma will have my hide if she finds out I told a lie," I whispered.

"Your ma knows we need the money. She won't question my decision on this," Pa replied.

As I looked up into my pa's face, I was sure that I saw tears. He looked so sad, and there was something else botherin' him that I just couldn't put my finger on.

Pa wrote down my name and age and then we walked to the mine entrance. The other men had already gone down into the mine. Pa lit our headlamps and we began to walk the mile into the earth. Soon there wasn't any light except for the small flame from our headlamps. I'd never been in a coal mine before. It was cold and damp.

When we got to a large wooden door, Pa told the man sitting on an old wooden box there that I was to take the man's place and that Mr. McClure was advancing the man to driving the mule that pulled the wagon of coal in and out of the mine.

"James, you're to sit on this box and pay attention for the mule driver to come out of the mine. The mine door has to remain tightly closed, except when a coal car is coming out. Ya see those pipes up there that go through the wall? They pump fresh air down to the miners, and if ya let the doors open too long, the fresh air will escape. The tunnels are built on a slope and the coal cars come hurtling down the track, so listen carefully for their rumbling because it is the only signal to open the door. Close the door just as soon as ya let the cars race through. Ya have to be quick 'bout it, ya hear? Don't make him wait," Pa explained.

Pa showed me how to open the big door and then he walked through it, to go deeper into the mine to do his daily task of digging coal. Once he walked away from me, I realized just how dark it is down there. At first I felt all grown up, sitting all alone in that dark, damp pit, but then I began hearing strange sounds and I became afraid of the things that I couldn't see. I had heard rumors of huge rats living inside the mine. I also wondered if the rats would bite me if I sat too still, so I began to move my feet to and fro. I did this until my legs began to get tired. Pa didn't tell me how long it would be until a wagon load of coal would be coming out of the mine, so I just waited and waited. It seemed like hours before I finally heard the mule's feet tappin' along the tracks.

I ran to open the door but it wouldn't budge. I pulled with all my might, but I just couldn't figure out how to get it to move. Finally, the mule driver pushed the door open from his side and I got some momentum to finish opening it wide enough for the mule and wagon to pass by me.

"What's wrong, boy? Ya weak or stupid?" the man shouted.

"Sorry, sir! I'll try harder next time," I replied.

"See that ya do. Listen for the clip-clop of the mule's feet comin' towards the door so ya can begin to pull straight away and not keep me a-waitin'. Time's money in this job and I don't plan to be losin' money due to a lazy boy. What's your name?" he bellowed.

"James Millward, sir", I replied.

"Ya be William's boy?" He asked.

"Yes, sir," I said.

"Well, maybe you'll be as good a worker as your ol' man someday. There be two of us drivin' mule today, so you'll be busy. Keep your ears open, and be quick about it. Your back will get stronger in a day or two."

The man was still talkin' as he walked behind the mule and wagon, but I didn't hear anything else that he said. I was so embarrassed that I hadn't been able to open the door fast enough. I began to wonder if the man would tell my pa. I'd surely get a whippin' if Pa heard about it. The rest of the day went by slowly. I did figure out the technique on how to get the big door to move faster, but I didn't like workin' in the mine. However, I'd never admit to anyone just how afraid I was in those first few hours.

Sittin' alone in the dark silence made fallin' asleep almost inevitable. No matter how hard I tried, my eyes wanted to close, but as soon as I heard the rumble of the mule and wagon comin' I got wide awake. I didn't want anyone else to have to reprimand me for not working fast enough.

The two men who were drivin' mule began callin' me Jimmy. No one had ever called me that, but it made me feel all grown up to get a nickname. Mum always called us by our Christian names. In the mine the men didn't stick to such formalities. I also heard a lot of other words that my mum wouldn't like. In fact, almost all of the men I saw on my first day at work cursed and spit tobacco.

I began to think of Mum. I wondered what she'd have to say 'bout Pa takin' me out of school. I didn't like goin' to school, but Ma said everyone needs an education. If I was gonna work in the mine, I didn't need to read and write.

I heard a whistle blowin' from outside of the mine, and soon a group of men came walkin' towards me.

"Hey, ya new here, aren't ya?" one man asked me.

"Yes, sir," I replied.

"Well, I bet you be glad to git outta here now," he said as he reached for the rope that pulled the big door open. I watch as he opened it; he didn't flinch one bit. Would I have muscles like that someday, I wondered.

I wasn't sure if I was supposed to wait there for Pa to come out of the mine or if I should go 'head and follow the other men out. I stood watchin' the men comin' and goin', each raisin' a hand to each other as they passed.

When my pa finally came into view, his face was black with coal dust. He slapped me on the shoulder and we walked side-by-side out of the coal mine. However, we didn't speak until we were away from all the other miners.

"How was ya first day, son?" Pa asked.

"It took me a few tries to git the door to swing open, but I figured out how to make it move faster. How long was we in the mine today, Pa?" I asked.

"Ya just worked a twelve-hour shift. Soon as ya git home, you'll wash up, eat supper, and go to bed. Tomorrow will be the same. We won't git a day off 'til Sunday," Pa replied.

I didn't have the energy to say anything more. It took all I had just to keep up with Pa's stride.

As we got nearer to our house, I saw people were sittin' on our swing out back. We rarely got company, and as we got closer I could see it was the O'Malleys. I was still smartin' about Patrick callin' Pa a scab, yet I wondered why his parents were on our swing.

When we got to our yard, Pa told me to go get washed and go into the house. I knew somethin' was really wrong, and I did as I was told at once. As I stood on the back porch washin' myself, I listened carefully to try and hear what was goin' on.

Pa talked in a soft voice, and then I heard Mrs. O'Malley begin to cry. Mr. O'Malley sounded mad. I looked around but I didn't see Patrick anywhere. I went into the kitchen. Mum was puttin' supper on the table.

"Mum, what's goin' on?" I asked.

"We'll talk 'bout it all later. Did ya have a hard day, son?" Ma said as she hugged me.

"I did good, Mum. Are ya mad that Pa took me into the mine?" I asked.

"I'll discuss it with your pa when we're alone, but I don't like ya bein' in the mine. You're just a boy. Now, if ya want to start eatin', go ahead. I know ya must be tired and hungry," Mum replied.

Usually we'd all sit down together when company was over, but this day was entirely different. This was no happy occasion. There was tension in the air even though I couldn't hear the conversation goin' on outside. I figured my pa would tell me what was happenin' on our way to work in the mornin', so I ate my supper and then took my plate to the sink for Sarah to wash.

"James, you'll be sleepin' on the floor in me and Pa's bedroom tonight. Go ahead and git yourself settled in. The O'Malleys will be in your bedroom," Mum said.

"Are they goin' to live with us now?" I asked.

"They'll just be here a short while, just until they can get another place of their own," Mum said as she began to cry.

Seeing the tears flow down Mum's face made me so sad. I didn't feel like a little boy anymore yet I didn't feel like a man, either. I just felt sad. I knew my fun-filled, childhood days were over.

CHAPTER THREE

ANNA MILLWARD

Thursday – April 2, 1891 – A Sorrowful Day

I got out of bed before daylight to get the fire going in the coal stove. I got the coffee started and packed William's lunch pail. Although I could use a bit more sleep, I always enjoy the early mornings before the children are awake. It's my time to think and pray. Soon I'll have another little one to nurse and my time will no longer be my own. As near as I can figure, the babe will be born in another month. We really can't afford another mouth to feed. At least I can nurse this new one, but six children is a larger family than I ever expected to have.

Before William left for work this morning he seemed quieter than usual. I could tell something was bothering him, yet I had so many things on my mind that I didn't think to ask about his concerns. I was thinking about what William had said about moving to Frye Hollow and about the coming weekend, when we could take the children there on a picnic.

I'd heard the rumors about the miners striking, but William didn't intend to be one of them. He'd told me many times that he planned to go to work each day and to mind his own business. When several of the women in the patch talked about the coming coal strike, each had her own opinion of what might happen, but I tried to keep my thoughts to myself. Like William, I didn't want any trouble.

James, Benjamin, and Sarah had just left for school when I heard someone calling my name from the back yard. Jacob and Delilah were still sleeping, so I rushed outside to see what was going on.

"Anna, can you come quickly to Colleen's house?" Gretchen Klink cried.

"I have to get my little ones up first. What's wrong?" I knew it must be something awful because nothing ever got Gretchen upset. Seeing her with tears rolling down her face frightened me. This big, German woman was always a pillar of strength, rarely showing emotion.

"Please, come as soon as you can. Colleen needs us" Gretchen said as she turned and ran back across the field which led to the company houses on First Street in the village of Central.

I awoke Jacob and Delilah and dressed them both as quickly as I could. However, I would not be able to run with a three-year-old and a five-year-old.

"Mama, where are we goin'?" Jacob asked.

"Colleen needs me. Miss Klink came to ask for my help," I replied.

"What kind of help, Mama?" Jacob asked.

"I'm not sure yet. You be a good boy and help me by watchin' Delilah."

As soon as I crossed the field and got closer to First Street, I could hear wailing and crying. Men I had never seen before were shouting, and people were running all around. Then I saw Colleen O'Malley and two of her children standing outside of her duplex house. Men were throwing their belongings out on the street. Colleen's husband, Peter, was being held back by two large men with badges on their coats.

"What's goin' on, Colleen?" I cried.

"The coal police are throwin' us out of our home. They said Peter was at the Morewood Mine last night, and any miner who wants to cause trouble can no longer live in a company-owned house," Colleen sobbed.

"Jacob, you stay right here and watch the baby. Do not move from my sight!" I said as I put Delilah down on the grass.

Within minutes, everything the O'Malleys owned was out of the house. Peter was pushed to the ground by the men who were holding him, and Colleen ran to his side.

"Oh, Peter, what shall we do?" Colleen sobbed.

"You'll bring all of your belongings and come home with me until we get this straightened out," I said.

"If we do that the mine owner may put you and William out of your home, too," Peter replied.

"Just come along with me now and we'll discuss everything with William when he gets home later," I whispered.

Peter and Colleen picked up as much of their things as they could carry, while I collected all four young'uns, and then we all walked back across the field. I didn't know where we'd find room for another family in our small abode, but I couldn't let our friends be standing out on the street with everyone staring and gossipin' about them. I knew William would have an idea of how to help.

I noticed Gretchen Klink carrying Colleen's rocking chair, which was loaded down with the O'Malleys' belongings. However, no one else tried to help. I suppose everyone was afraid of what would happen if they got involved in the matter. I myself was wondering what Peter had done to cause so much trouble for his family, but I didn't dare ask. I'd have to wait until all of the children were put down for bed tonight, and then we could discuss the events of this horrible day.

By the time we got to my house, Colleen had stopped cryin' but now she looked awfully mad. Peter wasn't talkin' at all, just hung his head as he walked slowly beside his wife up the back steps and into my kitchen.

"I'll make us all breakfast," I said.

Jacob was such a good little helper. He knew that somethin' was wrong so he offered to play with his little sister and Colleen's two little ones. Michael is four and Adel just two years old. The children were used to playing together— Colleen and I visited each other as often as we could and we helped each other all of the time, so the children didn't see today as being any different in that aspect.

"Anna, you don't have to do this," Peter said.

"Nonsense. You need some time to figure out where you'll go and what you'll be doin'. I know William will help you in any way he can. Just calm down and have breakfast and a spot of tea. We'll pray about the problems," I replied.

"I can't see any good comin' out of this, Anna," Colleen said as she began to cry again.

"Now, you just calm yourself, Colleen! Ain't no problem the Lord can't solve," I whispered as I hugged her.

I took three cups from my cupboard and put the hot water in my china teapot along with a tea ball filled with sassafras tea. The sweet smell filled the kitchen, reminding me of happier times that I'd had with Colleen, Gretchen Klink, and Elizabeth Danner.

When my first husband, Joseph, and I came to America from Wales in 1881 I don't think I could have made it through that first year here in Rocktown. These three women befriended me and Joseph and shared their hard-earned supplies with us. When Joseph was killed in the mine shortly after arriving here, I didn't know what to do. William had asked me to marry him, but I really depended on these women to help me deal with my grief.

"Anna, I don't think William will be very happy to see us here. I wasn't exactly kind to him yesterday, and now that the coal police have gotten involved it could be dangerous for you to have us in your home," Peter said.

"I've never known William to be anything but fair to people. I'm sure you both have a lot to tell each other when he gets home," I replied.

Gretchen knocked on the back door and then walked into the kitchen to join us.

"Here is your rockin' chair and clothes, Colleen. I'll go fetch some more of your things. I'm so sorry to see this happen to ya," Gretchen said.

"Thank you, Gretchen. We appreciate your help," Colleen replied.

It didn't seem like Colleen or Peter wanted to talk about their problem with anyone yet. Peter didn't look at Gretchen. I suppose he was embarrassed at being put out of his home, but then I thought of something else I'd heard. Was Peter involved directly in the strike?

"Would you like to stay for breakfast, Gretchen?" I asked.

"No, thank you. I'll just be goin' now," Gretchen said.

I prepared breakfast for us all and then Colleen helped me to clean up once we had all of the children fed. She and Peter went back to get more of their belongings. I put some quilts on the floor in the children's bedroom. The mile-long walk across the field to Colleen's house, along with the fresh spring air, made the children ready for an early nap.

As soon as I was sure they were all asleep, I went to my icebox to see what I could fix for supper. I'd have to make something that I could stretch to fill up eight children and four adults. There wasn't much in the icebox, but I remembered a smoked ham was hanging in the springhouse. I had plenty of potatoes in the root cellar, so I decided to make scalloped potatoes and ham. I still had a few jars of applesauce in the pantry to add to the meal.

It was soon time for my older children to be getting home from school. I'd made a batch of raisin cookies for them to have, to hold them over until their pa got home for supper. Colleen and Peter spent the afternoon carrying their things to our shed in the back yard. They were taking a rest on the swing under the grape arbor.

Benjamin and Sarah came rushing in the back door, both talking so fast that I couldn't understand a word they were saying.

"Children, one at a time, please. Now, what's got ya all excited?" I asked.

"Pa came to school this mornin' and took James to the mine," Benjamin replied.

"Yes, and Miss Hodgekiss was in a bad mood all day and didn't allow us to talk," Sarah said.

"You mean to tell me James isn't with you?" I asked.

"No, Mum, he's at the mine with Pa. Pa told Miss Hodgekiss that James won't be comin' back to school," Benjamin cried.

"Calm down now. I'm sure your pa's got a good explanation for what he's doin'. Come sit at the table and have a cookie. Sarah, would you please fetch the little ones from the bedroom where they be playin'?" I replied.

"Ma, what's Mr. and Mrs. O'Malley doin' on our swing? Why ain't he at the mine with Pa?" Benjamin asked.

"There was something goin' on at the mine last night that Mr. O'Malley will discuss with your pa after supper. The O'Malleys will be staying with us for tonight. I made up a bed on the floor of your bedroom for them to sleep. I want you children to stay out of the kitchen after the meal so as the men can talk. Will you help watch the wee ones for me, Benjamin?" I said.

"Yes, Mum," Benjamin replied.

Just then I heard Patrick O'Malley calling out to his parents as he came running through the field towards our house.

"Ma! Pa! What ya be doin' here? What happened to our house?" Patrick cried.

"Come sit with us awhile, son. We need to stay here for tonight. Tomorrow we'll find us a new home, and I'll be lookin' for a new job," Peter said.

I didn't mean to eavesdrop, but I couldn't help but hear what was being said as I worked in my little kitchen. Patrick began to cry, and then Peter put his arms around Colleen and Patrick. I watched as the three of them held each other close.

After all of the children finished their cookies, Sarah set the table for our evening meal. It wasn't often that we had company for supper, so she was singing as she worked. I loved to hear my daughter singing, but, oh, how sad I felt about the reason for this gathering. I was upset that William had taken James out of school and taken him to work at the mine without consulting me. We'd never talked about child labor before, but I'd been reading about the mines out east and how many children were actually dying while working as breaker-boys. I worried at what my little boy was doing in this mine of Western Pennsylvania.

It seemed like hours before it was time for William to get home from work. Twelve hours in the dark, cold mine was hard on my husband. I wondered how it would be for a small boy of only nine years old.

"Sarah, I think it would be best if I get all of the little ones fed and ready for bed, and then when your pa gets home the adults can eat together. Will you please help me with them?" Anna asked.

"Yes, Mum," Sarah replied.

It didn't take us long to have all four of the children washed up for dinner and seated at my kitchen table. I didn't think Colleen would mind that I'd taken charge of her children, since she seemed to still be in shock from the events of the morning.

I had just finished getting everyone's faces wiped off after their dinner when I heard William's voice. James came into the kitchen.

"Mum, what's goin' on?' he asked.

CHAPTER FOUR

WILLIAM MILLWARD

Thursday – April 2, 1891 – The Morewood Massacre

It was a surprise to see Colleen and Peter O'Malley in my back yard as me and James walked home from the mine on April 2. I'd already heard part of what had happened, and although I didn't want to be involved in the strike or the miner's march, it appeared that Peter O'Malley had brought the trouble to my doorstep.

"James, go on in the house. I'll be in shortly," I said to my son.

"Hello, Peter! Mind tellin' me what happened?" I asked.

"Late last night the strikers were holding a meeting at the Standard Works. When the meetin' broke up at around two or three in the morning, a large crowd of people, accompanied by a marching band, began to march down Alverton Road toward the Morewood Works. Morris Pigman, manager of the Standard company store, and John Hart, boss at the Standard Mine, said that the strikers cut the telegraph wires at the Standard company store so that no warning could be sent to the Morewood Works. When the men reached the company store at Morewood there were deputies on duty. Then they continued down the road toward the gates of the works where Captain Loar and his twelve men were stationed. Captain Loar and his men shot two rounds into the crowd, killin' six of the marching miners. Three other miners were lyin' in the street bleedin'. It was awful," Peter cried.

"Who was killed?" I asked.

"They took seven bodies to the undertaker's stable. Four Hungarians were killed. Paul Dohannis of Standard Mine was shot in the head and died at the company store. Valentine Zeidel of Donnelly Mine was shot through the neck. Josef Brochto of Tarrs was shot through the chest. Jacob Shucaskey of Tarrs was shot through the head. William, he has a wife and five children in Poland, just a-waitin' for him to send money so they can come to America." Peter stopped talkin' and wiped tears from his face. "John Fudora of Standard Mine was shot about his left eye. Antonio Adna-Rist of Standard Mine was shot through the head and Cresezo Buero of Tarrs was shot in the chest. There were more men shot, but I don't know if they're dead or just injured," Peter said.

"Peter, I'm really sorry to hear 'bout this. I had a bad feelin' 'bout strikin'. I know how the men feel about those of us who want to keep on workin', but I have a family to raise and so do you. When I got to work this mornin' Mr. McClure asked me if I had a son old enough to work. He didn't tell us 'bout the trouble at the Morewood Mine, but we knew somethin' was goin' on. I took James out of school today to work in the mine. Several other men did the same. I heard ya lost your job. Is that true?" I asked.

"Aye! Not only my job, but the coal police threw us out of our house. Me and Colleen spent the day pickin' our stuff up off the road and bringin' it here to your shed. Anna said we could stay here for the night. Tomorrow we'll be movin' on, but I don't know where we'll go. I don't think I'll get a job in any of the mines around here," Peter whispered.

"Let's go on in and eat dinner. We'll talk more after the young'uns are asleep. No sense worryin' 'em 'bout this trouble," I replied as I turned towards the house.

Anna must have been watchin' for me 'cause she was already on the back porch, standin' at the ol' galvanized tub with a bucket of hot water. I washed the dirt from my face and hands and then went into the kitchen.

Anna got the children all fed and put down to bed for the night. I'm sure that she was tired and very worried about the events of the day.

"William, would you please say grace?" Anna said.

I knew by the sound of her voice that once dinner was over Anna would have words for me. I guess I couldn't blame her. I'd made the decision to take our oldest son out of school and then get him a job in the mine. I had also tried to keep some of the problems that were going on in our community from her. I didn't know how much Anna was told today about the strike, or the discontent among the miners, but I was sure that she could put it all together.

"Bless us, Lord, and thank Thee for this food. Bless the hands that made this food. Lord, help our friends and neighbors on this dark day. Bless all the souls who have died or are dying. Amen," I prayed.

"Thank you, Anna and William, for givin' us a place to lay our heads this night," Colleen said.

"I'm beholden to ya, William," Peter whispered.

"You'd do the same for us, wouldn't you, Peter?" I asked.

"Aye, that I would," Peter replied.

The rest of the meal was eaten in complete silence. Peter and Colleen had no idea of where they'd go, and my thoughts were on the Morewood Massacre that had taken place this morning. I was also thinking of the question I'd just put to Peter O'Malley: Would you do the same for us, Peter? I didn't believe that Peter would continue to be my friend. I'd seen men turn on each other when the union went against non-union workers. I'd even seen brother against brother.

"Anna, you must be exhausted! I'll do the dishes and clean up the kitchen. You and William can go to bed. Peter will help me. Won't you, Peter?" Colleen said.

"Yes, that's a good idea," Peter replied.

"Thank you! I'll take you up on this offer. I'm very tired. If you need anything, just call out," Anna replied, as she stood up and rubbed the small of her back.

I just nodded as I rose from my chair and followed Anna into the bedroom. I was preparing myself for the anger I'd seen all evening on Anna's face, but once we got into bed, Anna turned her back to me. I leaned over her to kiss her goodnight and saw tears on her face, glistening in the moonlight.

"Aw, Anna. Please don't cry," I said.

"We'll talk tomorrow when no one is here. Are you takin' James to work again tomorrow?" Anna asked.

"Yes!" I replied.

Anna didn't want to argue, for fear that the O'Malleys would hear, but I knew that she was planning her words carefully with what she'd say to me tomorrow. The twinge in her side caused her to move farther away from me. I could tell that she was so uncomfortable sleeping on her side, but she didn't want to snuggle close.

My thoughts turned to my own childhood back in Wales. I'd gone to work in the mines at a young age and so had my brother Joseph. Mining was hard work and there was never enough money to live on.

It was not an easy decision to take James into the mine today, but it had to be done. Having a large family is a blessing but also a curse. The mine owners are cutting wages.

In December 1890, twenty percent of H.C. Frick's coke operations were shut down due to a lack of demand for coke.

I could hear whispers coming from the bedroom the O'Malley family occupied. Angry whispers, sniffles, and then footsteps going from the bedroom outside to the porch. Soon all was quiet, except for the gentle snoring of my son James.

I had no idea how many families had been evicted today but I knew that if I continued to shelter the O'Malleys I, too, would have trouble with Mr. McClure or the coal police. It would be best for everyone if they went to another town and tried to make a fresh start.

The homestead in Frye Hollow was looking better to me. It was going to be hard, becoming independent of the coal company, but in the long run we'd be better off. I had a good work record, and I was always honest with Mr. McClure. I figured I'd work at the mine as long as I could, and then I'd try to get settled into the farmhouse before the fall. If Anna could get a garden in and sell some produce, we'd maybe be able to purchase a milk cow.

I couldn't go to sleep with all of the things that were going around in my head. Even though I knew the morning would be here far too soon, I wondered about the future of my family. I was also worried about the families of the men who had been killed on Morewood Street. Anyone who had a wife and family living in a company-owned house would be evicted just as quickly as the O'Malleys had been put out.

How many women and children will suffer because of this strike, I wondered.

It wasn't uncommon for evicted people to join other families and to become extended families. Sometimes they even had to separate their children, giving one or two to different relatives while they searched for a place to live. In the event that the husband was killed, their widows may never recover financially, never be able to return to their homeland. I thought back to the time when I first read the post, back in Wales, about coming to America.

COME TO AMERICA!

WE OFFER YOU LAND,

HOUSING, AND A FAIR WAGE!

WE EVEN PAY YOUR PASSAGE TO AMERICA!

Well, the coal company did pay my passage to America, albeit in the bowels of a ship with only rice and water to eat on the journey. The housing I took as a boarder only gave me a small cot to sleep upon, porridge for breakfast, and soup for dinner.

When I married Anna we continued to live in the company-owned house that she and Joseph had leased. We would never own the house or the land. So the advertisements that the coal companies put up in many other countries were untrue. They didn't give a man anything.

Anna turned out to be the best thing that ever happened to me. I'd proposed marriage to help her when my brother was killed, but she was the one helping me. Gone were all of my lonely nights. We have been good for each other, and I'd do everything in my power to make her happy.

However, right now, I knew that Anna was not happy with me or with the situation that had befallen her best friend. Tomorrow would be another hard day for my wife. I feared that she would have to say goodbye to Colleen O'Malley. There was no other way to get around it.

It seemed that I had no sooner fallen asleep than I heard someone stumbling up the back steps.

I got out of bed and stepped around my children, who were lying on the floor. I opened the back door to find Peter O'Malley lying in the grass just beyond our back porch.

"Peter, what are ya doin?" I asked.

"Oh, William! Ya ol' goody two-shoes! I just come from LaLa's Tavern. Had me a few pints," Peter slurred.

"Git in the house and go to sleep. You'll wake the children!" I whispered.

"I'll be leavin' before they git up. Don't want to be beholden to no scab," Peter replied.

"Peter, you're makin' me mad. You're drunk and you're rude. Go sleep on the swing," I said as I turned and went back to bed.

I'd no sooner fallen asleep than it was time to get up for work. I heard someone go out the back door, slamming it as they went. Anna heard the door, too, and she got up to get breakfast for me and James.

Colleen came out of the bedroom and looked around the kitchen. Her eyes were red and swollen.

"Anna, have ya seen Peter and Patrick this mornin'?" Colleen asked.

"No, I haven't seen them since I've been up," Anna replied.

"They're both gone already," Colleen said as she turned to go back into the bedroom.

I didn't see that it would do any good to tell Colleen that her husband had been out all night and had come home drunk early this morning. She had enough to worry about, and I was still angry about Peter's comment. James and I ate our breakfast in silence and then walked to work.

We were just goin' into the mine when I heard someone call out my name.

"William, hold up a minute. I want a word with ya," Mr. McClure said.

"Go on to your post, James. Ya know what to do, don't ya?" I asked.

"Yes, Pa. I'll see ya tonight," James replied.

I walked back to meet Mr. McClure, hoping he wasn't going fire me because I'd taken in the O'Malleys.

"You're a good worker, William, and I appreciate ya bringin' your boy to work when we're short on men that want to work. I just don't want to see ya get in the middle of anythin', so ya don't have to tell me nothin' if ya don't want to, but I heard the O'Malley family is stayin' at your place. Is that true?" Mr. McClure asked.

"They stayed the night with us, but Peter left early this mornin' to look for work in another town. He said he'll be sendin' for his wife and children as soon as he finds a job and a place to live. I don't want any part of what Peter's been up to, and I won't cause ya no trouble," I replied.

"Good to hear that from ya, William. How's the boy like workin' as a nipper?" Mr. McClure asked.

"He's doin' just fine."

"Well, the sooner ya git the O'Malleys out of your house, the better off you'll be. I know you're a good man, but I can't say what the men who are strikin' will do if they think you're takin' sides. I've always thought that the Irish were influenced by the Molly Maguires. Troublemakers, the whole lot of 'em," Mr. McClure said.

"Now, Mr. McClure, there's not a one of the Molly Maguires left 'round here. That's all just rumor stirred up by all the other ethnic groups. O'Malley and his family have been here as long as I have—goin' on twelve years—and he's never caused trouble before," I replied.

"Well, for your sake, I hope he takes his family with him. Not right for a man to expect someone else to take care of his family," Mr. McClure said as he turned and walked away.

I got the message Mr. McClure was givin' me. I sure hoped Peter would find work soon.

CHAPTER FIVE

COLLEEN O'MALLEY

Thursday – April 2, 1891 – Life Changes

Peter was turning into someone I no longer knew or trusted. He'd been keepin' secrets from me for weeks. I saw him talkin' to men from other minin' towns. I heard him tellin' Patrick about the men strikin' and about the Pinkerton agents keepin' watch over all the mines in our area. I just couldn't believe that the man I loved would turn on his friends and co-workers.

When the coal police came beatin' on my door, I knew it was because of Peter goin' out late last night. Peter had come home very early this mornin' and he had been white as a sheet. He wouldn't answer any of my questions before he left for work.

The coal police didn't wait for me to answer the door, they just burst right in and yelled: "You're bein' evicted. Get out at once."

Peter was right behind the coal police, and they pushed him to the ground. One man put his foot on Peter's back and held him in place while the others ran in and out of our home, taking everything that wasn't nailed down and throwing it haphazardly into the street.

I knew most of my neighbors were watchin' what was goin' on, but I didn't see Gretchen Klink until she came a-runnin', with Anna Millward followin' behind her. My two best friends watched as all of our personal belongings were thrown out into the street. All I could do was hold Adel and Michael in my arms. Adel is only two years old and cried because her Momma was cryin', but Michael is four and old enough to know somethin' was very wrong. He was so frightened by the coal police. We were all three cryin' when Anna came and put her arms around me.

"Anna, what will I do?" I cried.

"Colleen, you'll come to my house for now. We'll figure somethin' out, for sure," Anna replied.

Anna whispered somethin' to her son Jacob and he reached up and took Michael from me. Then Anna took Adel and carried her on one hip with her own wee one on her other hip. Anna's protruding stomach looked bigger than a watermelon in late summer as she walked across the road and into the field that led to her and William's house.

I picked up as many things as I could carry and followed Anna. Gretchen gave a nod of her head as she began to load our blankets onto my rockin' chair. The coal police let Peter up from the ground as soon as they'd finished clearin' out the house. We didn't own much, but it was more than we could carry. Peter gathered as much of the children's things as he could hold and followed behind us.

Behind me, I heard Elizabeth Danner yellin' somethin' and then I heard someone sayin': "Don't get involved or you'll get evicted, too!"

I'd been friends and neighbors with the Danners since me and Peter had come to America from Ireland. We'd met at Ellis Island when our ships landed around the same time, back in 1880. The Danners were from England, and Daniel had also been a miner in his homeland.

What would we do now? We had very little money saved and no place to go. We couldn't stay with our neighbors. They were in the same situation as us: The coal and coke company owned everything and we were all indebted to them, much like the slaves of the South. At first, we had believed that America would be a better place to live, but it soon became clear that the very people who had promised us a better life were exploiting us for their own profit.

The day passed by ever so slowly. Peter walked back and forth, carrying our meager belongings to the Millwards' little shed. Anna insisted that we put everything inside the shed and make ourselves at home with her and William until we could figure out a plan for what to do next.

As the day wore on my fear turned to sadness, then to anger. What had my husband done? All of these years he'd been a hard-working and honest man that had made me proud. What had changed him?

"Colleen, we need to talk. Come sit on the swing with me," Peter said as we finally got the last of our things put away in the shed.

"Yes! I want answers, Peter! What did you do?" I cried.

"I didn't want to worry you with the details, but I've been meetin' with the miners from our area for months now. The coal-and-coke barons are robbin' us blind. We can never get ahead as long as we're being paid by script. We don't own anything. Not our home or land; not even the clothes on our backs. They make us promises but never follow through. We're workin' in unsafe conditions for twelve hours a day. They force us to rob timbers to save themselves money, only to make our jobs even more dangerous. It's time the miners stand together and force a change before more men die," Peter explained.

"Why couldn't you just keep your mouth shut? Let someone else do the strikin'," I cried.

"Colleen, who else? Tell me who will do it if not for the very men who are doin' the work!" Peter shouted.

"Lower your voice! Isn't it bad enough that the whole neighborhood has watched as we were thrown out of our home?" I whispered.

Peter put his hands on his knees and lowered his head to his hands. We sat quietly until we heard voices coming from across the field. It was William and his oldest son, James. Peter wasn't sure if William would also throw us out. He couldn't blame William if he did. After all, they weren't exactly in agreement about the coming strike.

"Evenin', Peter, Colleen. James, you go on in and tell your mum I'll be in shortly," William said.

"Colleen, go on in with Anna," Peter said.

I admired that Anna had pulled together enough food from her pantry for two families to have their fill. The youngest children ate their dinner and chatted to each other like it was a holiday. However, James and Patrick wouldn't even look at each other. I watched the two oldest boys pick at their plates in an uneasy silence.

"James, you've had a long day. Why don't you get to bed early tonight," Anna said.

"I plan to, Mum," James replied.

Anna took her four youngest children into the bedroom and got them all settled down for the night.

I took Adel and Michael into the other bedroom and tucked them in. Patrick came into the bedroom and offered to tell the little ones a story. As he got down on the floor I noticed that he had tears in his eyes.

"Are ya turnin' in for the night as well, Patrick?" I asked.

"Yes, Mum. Good night," he replied.

I went out to the kitchen where Anna sat at the table, sippin' a cup of tea.

"Anna, how can I thank ya? I don't know what we'll do now," I said.

"The men will figure somethin' out," Anna replied.

Peter and William came into the kitchen and ate their dinner without saying a word.

I offered to do the dishes and clean the kitchen so Anna and William could go to bed. Anna was getting close to having her baby, and I'm sure cooking for all of us was quite a chore for her. I also knew that Anna had many questions to ask her husband, too. She didn't need to tell me that she was unhappy about William taking their son out of school to work in the mine. I could understand her concern for James. He's still a child, only nine years old. What was happening to our husbands? Was everyone going mad?

"Thank you, Colleen. I'll take you up on that offer. I really am tired," Anna replied.

As soon as Anna stood up, William did, too, and they both went into their bedroom. I finished the chores and then went to bed. Peter was already in bed.

"Peter, what is goin' on?" I cried.

"Tomorrow I'll be goin' to Connellsville to seek employment with the railroad or whatever I can find. I'll not get another position in any of the mines. I hear that Connellsville is known as the 'Coke Capital' due to the amount and quality of coke produced in the city's many beehive ovens. The Pittsburgh steel mills need that coke and I need to work. The railroad seems like the best place to start lookin' for a job," Peter whispered.

"What about our friends, the Millwards?" I asked.

"Right now I don't think William or James want us to stay here. They could be out of work, too, if the company thinks they be a-sidin' with us. Besides, I fear there are hard feelings now. Patrick called William a damn scab in front of James, and now with James goin' to work in the mine it's gotten out of control," Peter whispered.

"Peter, you have to make this right. Did ya tell the boy to apologize?" I cried.

"I can't tell 'im to say somethin' he don't mean. We'll talk tomorrow evening," Peter said as he rolled over, putting his back to me.

"Peter O'Malley, you will not dismiss me this way. I insist you and Patrick both say you're sorry to the Millwards," I hissed through clenched teeth.

"Woman, mind your words!"

Peter had never spoken so venomously to me. I got up from bed and checked the children. Patrick was lying on his back, staring straight up at the ceiling, but didn't say a word as I bent to kiss his forehead goodnight. I returned to the bed, curled up in the fetal position, and cried myself to sleep.

When the baby awoke early the next morning, Peter was already gone. I was so angry that I had no say in the matter of what was to become of our family, but I knew that a significant change was in the making. I took Adel into the kitchen, where Anna was preparing breakfast.

"Has William gone to work already?" I asked.

"Yes, he and James left just a while ago. I heard Peter leaving long before the others awoke," Anna replied.

"He's goin' to seek work in Connellsville. I don't know where we'll live, but we'll be leavin' as soon as possible," I whispered.

"I'll do all I can for ya, Colleen. You're my best friend and I hate to see ya leave, but there's nothin' here for ya now," Anna whispered in return.

All of the children came into the kitchen just then, ready for their breakfast. Anna had made a large pot of oatmeal, enough for all to eat their fill. I was glad for the distraction because I knew that if I tried to talk I'd end up crying again. Anger seemed to consume me. I couldn't even pray that morning. It was the first time that I'd ever distrusted my husband. Then I began to think about Anna, about what all of this was doing to her.

Anna's son had had to go to work inside the mine and she had told me that her husband William was also acting strange. There was an underlying current of something brewing among all of the miners and their families. The friendships that had been made when we all first came to America were slipping away. Talk of strikes, unions, and child labor tormented almost every family. Gone were all of the promises that had been made years ago by the coal companies. There was no money. Just the gray, dirty streets of the coal patch towns, and tiresome, backbreaking work.

CHAPTER SIX

PATRICK O'MALLEY

Wednesday –April 1, 1891 –Lost Child

I thought about the events from a few nights ago. I was helpin' Pa carry coal from our shed to the coal bin on the back porch and he told me all 'bout his plans. Pa talked like he was excited about helpin' the men plan the march to Morewood. He also told me to watch what I said to James at school, 'cause he might just be a damn scab, just like his pa.

Pa also made me promise to keep our talks a secret from Ma. He said she'd get mad if she knew how he really felt about William Millward.

"No sense talkin' to men who don't want to help themselves," Pa said.

So, I tried not to talk with James at school, but on the way home I saw James and his little brother Benjamin goin' to the fishin' hole. I figured I'd see what they knew 'bout the things my pa had discussed with me. I bet they didn't even know 'bout the way their pa was a coward.

"My pa says your pa's a scab!" I shouted at the Millward boys.

"What are ya talkin''bout, Patrick?" James asked.

"Guess your pa don't think ya be man enough to talk to 'bout the mine, but my pa says he's gonna help all the men get more money by startin' a strike. He says your pa don't want to help. Is that right?" I shouted.

"Don't know nothin' 'bout no strike, but my pa is no scab," James shouted back.

"Come on, Benjamin, let's go home," James said as he pulled in his fishin' line.

"Go ahead and run home to ya ma. I don't need a friend who's the son of a scab," I yelled.

James and his little brother practically ran all the way home from the fishin' hole. I sure did show them. My pa treats me like a man. I felt all grown up just knowin' that somethin' was gonna happen real soon.

When I got home, Ma was puttin' cookies on a plate for me and my little brother Michael. Baby Adel was takin' a nap so we had to be real quiet. After our snack, I took Michael outside to play. It wasn't somethin' I wanted to do, but Ma expected my help. I didn't like to watch my little brother, but I knew Pa would take me to the woodshed if I didn't do as Ma asked.

It was getting real late when Ma finally called us in to eat supper.

"Where's Pa?" I asked.

"I don't know. He hasn't come home from work. I suppose he could have stopped at the tavern on his way home," Ma said.

I could tell she was mad by the sound of her voice. Ma didn't take kindly to men goin' to the tavern. She didn't believe in drinkin'. My pa had been late comin' home from work a lot lately, and he never told Ma where he was. I'd heard them arguin' 'bout it, and Pa shouted at Ma a lot, too.

When the moon was high over the slate dump, Ma told me and Michael to get to bed. I didn't ever remember my pa havin' been out this late. I listened as Ma rocked on the old rockin' chair in the livin' room and I was sure I heard her cryin'. Best I go to sleep and mind my own business. If Pa was doin' any strikin' tonight I sure wasn't gonna be the one to let my ma know 'bout it. I sure hoped Pa would tell me all 'bout it tomorrow.

Thursday –April 2, 1891

When Ma woke me for school, her eyes were red and swollen. I didn't see any sign that my pa had come home yet. Although I didn't want to go to school today, I knew Ma was in no mood to hear excuses.

Mr. Millward came to the school early on and took James with him. He told Miss Hodgekiss that James wouldn't be comin' back to school.

As soon as school was over I ran home as fast as I could, only to find that no one was there and the house was emptied out.

"Ya folks be at the Millward house, Patrick," Mrs. Danner called from across the road.

I didn't wait to ask her any questions, I just ran as fast as I could to James's house. After all that Pa had said about William Millward, I wondered why my whole family would be over there. Then I remembered that my pa still hadn't come home from work and I got real worried.

When I got to James's house, my parents were sittin' on the swing under the grape arbor. Ma was cryin' again, and Pa had his elbows restin' on his knees with his head in his hands.

"Pa, what happened?" I cried.

"Patrick, many men died today. It's a sorrowful time for us all. Just don't talk 'bout anythin' I told ya. Keep ya mouth shut, boy!" Pa shouted.

"Peter, why are ya talkin' so harshly to our son? He's got nothin' to do with all this!" Ma cried.

"Patrick, Mrs. Millward has some cookies and milk for ya. Go in and see her, please," Ma whispered.

"I don't want no cookies, Ma. What's wrong?!" I cried.

"Listen to ya ma, boy!" Pa shouted.

I turned and ran behind the Millwards' woodshed. I wouldn't go inside until Ma and Pa went in, too. I sat down in the grass and tried to figure out what could have happened during the night.

Miss Hodgekiss had been actin' strange all day and she hadn't let anyone go outside to play at recess. Our home was empty, my parents were mad, and somehow we'd ended up at the Millwards', the last place I would have expected my pa to come.

I didn't want to go into the Millwards' house for supper, but when I heard Mrs. Millward callin' my name I figured I'd better go in or my pa would have my hide.

When I went inside, Mrs. Millward was so nice to me that I almost felt guilty for bein' so mean to James and Benjamin. Although the food sure did smell good, I didn't have much of an appetite. James was sittin' across the table from me, so I kept my eyes down and tried not to look at him.

I kept wonderin' if Pa had changed his mind about Mr. Millward, since we were all gonna stay here for the night. I knew my ma and Mrs. Millward were best friends, but how did Mr. Millward feel about my pa?

It was all so confusing. I just wished my pa would come and talk to me, because I didn't know what to say to the Millwards.

"Patrick, don't you like my cookin'?" Mrs. Millward asked.

"I'm just not very hungry," I replied.

Just then my ma came into the house and took my little brother and sister into the bedroom that we'd be sharin'.

"Ma, I'll tell Adel and Michael a story," I said.

I didn't want to be around the Millward boys, anyway. After my little brother and sister fell asleep, I tried to hear what was bein' said at the dinner table between my pa and Mr. Millward, but I realized that they weren't talkin' to each other either. Just like me and James, I guessed they weren't even lookin' at each other.

I heard my ma offer to clean up the kitchen, and then Mr. and Mrs. Millward went into the other bedroom.

My pa came in and lay down on the bed. He didn't say anything to me, so I pretended to be asleep. When Ma was finished in the kitchen she came into the bedroom and asked my pa what was goin' on. I'd never heard my pa talk so mean to my ma before. I hated to hear my parents argue, and I knew that we were in serious trouble. I just lay there, staring up at the ceiling, feelin' sick to my stomach. Ma got up and checked on the two little ones and then she kissed me on the forehead and got back into bed. The last thing I heard before I fell asleep was my ma, cryin'.

My pa awoke the next morning and didn't realize that he'd almost stepped on my head, getting quietly out of bed long before sunup. I watched from my spot on the floor while he pulled on his work pants and tiptoed to the back porch, where his work boots were. He didn't say a word to Ma, but just up and left.

I hadn't taken off my clothes the night before, since me and the little ones were sleepin' on a bed of quilts on the floor. I jumped up and followed my pa, to see what he was goin' to do. I watched as Pa sprinted up Rocktown Road towards the railroad tracks and then he headed towards Tarrs. I ran as fast as I could to keep up with him, but he was getting' farther and farther ahead of me.

"Pa, wait for me," I shouted.

"What are ya doin' here, Patrick?" Pa asked.

"I want to come with ya. James is workin' with his pa now, so I'll work, too," I replied.

"Ya just git on back home! I don't know where I'll end up findin' work, and ya will just hold me up," Pa shouted.

"But Pa . . ."

I heard the train comin' down the tracks, and then I watched as my pa swung himself up on the coal car. Soon the train was far out of sight. Pa had left us! I didn't want to live with the Millward family. Ma could do what she wanted, but I was gonna go with my pa and get a job.

I figured another train would be comin' soon, so I walked on the railroad ties towards that coal patch town of Old Bethany. It wasn't long until I heard the train blowin' its whistle back at the Tarrs crossing, so I stepped off of the tracks and waited to jump one of the coal cars as soon as the engine was around the bend and the conductor wouldn't see me hitchin' a ride, just like my pa had done earlier.

This train seemed to be goin' much faster than the one my pa had jumped on. I got as close to the track as I could, waiting for the exact moment when I could just reach up and grab hold of the ladder on the coal car. Pa made it look real easy. I was stretchin' as high as I could, reachin' for that ladder, and then I felt my foot trip on one of the railroad ties . . .

"Pa, help me! Oh, God, please help me!"

I hadn't prayed in a very long time, and I tried to reach up as the caboose was passin' over me, and then the pain gave way to a roarin' in my head. I was driftin' up to the clouds, like God was liftin' me up . . .

THE RAILROAD CREW

Thursday –April 2, 1891

As the train came 'round the first bend from the Tarrs crossin', the flagman Carl Gretz saw a small boy lyin' face down in the cinders beside the railroad tracks. It looked like one of his legs was missin' and his body rested in a pool of blood. Carl pulled the brake whistle to signal to the engineer to stop the train. Three quick blasts of the whistle to signal an emergency stop was needed. As soon as Carl felt the air brakes kick in he jumped down from the caboose and ran back to the injured child.

Harry Jarvens, the brakeman, was in the engine with the engineer, Rick Polasky.

"Go check with Carl to see what's wrong," Rick said.

"Sure don't need more delays this mornin," Harry replied.

Harry jumped down from the train and ran back towards the caboose. As he got closer he saw that Carl was bent over and pickin' somethin' up from the tracks. The closer he got the more he began to have a sick feelin' in his stomach. Carl turned and was holdin' a small boy in his arms. Blood was flowing' from the end of the child's thigh, the bottom half of his leg was gone.

"What the hell happened?" Harry cried.

"I didn't see it happen but apparently the kid was on the tracks. He's bleedin' real bad. Harry, give me your belt to wrap 'round his leg," Carl replied.

Harry took off his belt and pulled his dirty, red bandana from his back pocket and wrapped it 'round the stump of the child's leg, and then both men got into the caboose and gave the signal for Rick to start the train again. Harry pulled the whistle in Morse code to tell the engineer to hurry.

"Is he alive?" Harry asked.

"Yeah, but he's losin' a lot of blood. Looks like his left foot is crushed, too," Carl replied.

"Do ya know this kid?' Harry asked.

"No, never seen 'im before. Sure is a little thing. Too young to be out walkin' the tracks alone, that's for sure," Carl replied.

Both men rode the rest of the way to the Scottdale station in silence. Harry leaned out of the caboose window and vomited. Carl, who had laid the child on a cot, got down on his knees and began to pray. He knew there was a doctor in Scottdale, just a few streets up from the railroad station, but he also knew that only God could save this child.

CHAPTER SEVEN

WILLIAM MILLWARD

Friday– April 3, 1891 – The Scab

I didn't want to have words with Peter in front of the women or children, but I did plan to tell Peter what I thought of this situation. I'd seen this very thing happen at other mines. It always seemed that the men with the money won. H. C. Frick had called on the aid of the Pinkertons and the coal police to keep the miners in line. Rumors had been goin' fast and furious ever since the mine disaster at the Mammoth mine on January 27, 1891.

I woke James up early so we could eat a hot breakfast and leave for work before anyone else arose to ask questions. I didn't want to argue with Anna while the O'Malleys were in the house. It would have been better for us all if Anna hadn't insisted on helping them, but I really wasn't angry that she did. I was just worried about what would happen at the mine today. After all, I'd be crossing the picket lines with our son if the other miners continued to strike.

"Pa, what is Mr. O'Malley gonna do?" James asked as we walked the path to the mine.

"He'll try to find work in another town, doin' somethin' other than coal minin'. Now that he's involved in the strike the other mine owners will not hire him. I guess he can go talk to the railroad men in Connellsville," I replied.

"Pa, what caused the mine to explode at Mammoth?"
James asked.

"How do ya know 'bout that, son?" I asked.

"I heard someone say the mine ain't no place for a boy to
work, and they said men were makin' their boys be scabs. Is
it true, Pa? Am I a scab?" James asked.

"Son, don't pay no mind to what men or boys be a-sayin'.
We've got to take care of our own. Life is hard in a mining
town, and if everyone stops workin' and no one is minin' the
coal, we don't eat. I just want to work and take care of my
family. I seek no trouble with others. As for the Mammoth
mine disaster, the firedamp was ignited by a miner's oil
lamp, resulting in the deaths of 109 men and boys just after
9:00 a.m. in the Mammoth No. 1 mine in Mount Pleasant
Township, Westmoreland County, Pennsylvania."

"Pa, what's firedamp?" James asked.

"Firedamp is a flammable gas, also called methane, found
in coal mines. The gas accumulates in pockets in the coal,
and when the men drill it can release the gas and trigger
explosions," I explained.

"Did everyone blow up?" James asked.

"Most of the miners were not killed by the force of the
explosion, but rather were suffocated by the effects of the
afterdamp, or gas. The miners were mostly Polish, Hungarian,
and Italian immigrants who were killed that day. Seventy-
nine of the victims were buried in a mass grave at St. John the
Baptist Cemetery in Scottdale. The Mammoth mine incident
prompted Pennsylvania state legislation to strengthen mine
safety inspections, but no one is inspectin' the Central mine
yet. That's part of the reason O'Malley and many other miners
want to strike. They all want better workin' conditions and
better pay," I replied.

"Pa, I don't want ya to blow up," James whispered.

"Don't ya worry, son. I'll be careful. Ya just do the best ya can, and don't talk to no one about this. We just go to work do our job and come home at night. No reason to be goin' over it with the others. If any man or boy calls ya a scab, ya hold ya head up high and ya walk right past 'em. We mind our own business and do an honest day's work. Ya understand, boy?" I asked.

"Yes, sir!" James replied.

We walked the rest of the way to the mine in silence. When we came in sight of the mine yard, there were men and boys goin' into the lantern house. I was glad to see that there were still men willing to work. We were all in the same situation: having a family to raise and needing to provide for them as best we could. If that meant being called a "scab," then so be it.

Edek Pulaski and his twin brother, Dorek, came out of the lantern house just as me and James were about to go in to refill our headlamps.

"Mornin', William!" Edek said as we passed each other.

"Mornin' to you also, Brothers Pulaski," I said, addressing both men.

"This be ya oldest son, William?" Edek asked.

"Yes. He's the oldest," I replied.

"Didn't think you'd have a boy of twelve already. Small for his age, aye?" Dorek replied.

James looked from me to the men, and then lowered his head. He seemed to stand up as tall as he could, probably to appear older.

"Mind ya business, Pulaski! My son's old enough to work. That's all anyone needs to know," I stated.

"Hey, don't get yourself in a huff. Just makin' conversation. My boy Oles is twenty-one now, but he's been workin' in the mine for quite awhile. I know the hardships, I'll not be judgin' ya," Dorek replied.

James and I entered the lantern house without sayin' anything more to the men that I'd worked with for the past eleven years. The Pulaski brothers had come to America from Poland around the same time that I'd come from Wales. I always thought Dorek to be the peacemaker of the two brothers. Edek seemed to carry a grudge against people of other nationalities, which sometimes caused disputes. He especially disliked the German and Russian people, probably due to the wars waged in his old country. However, I'd never had any trouble with these men.

Anna became friends with Dorek's wife, Fela, and Edek's wife, Yvonne, shortly after she arrived in America back in 1881. The women often worked together, canning vegetables and cooking ethnic dishes. It helped me, to think of how these hard-working women kept harmony in the coal patch town of Central, and it calmed me to think of the good things instead of dwelling on the past few days.

I got the carbide for our headlamps, signed the ledger sheet, and turned to go to the mine. James stayed so close to me that I almost tripped over him. Once we were outside I showed James how to unscrew the lantern from his cap and fill it with the carbide and water. I also taught him how to keep the valve adjusted to keep the flame bright enough so that he could see when in the damp, dark mine.

Several other men were walking to the mine entrance, yet no one seemed to be in the mood for talking. The coal police were still meandering around the yard office, but there didn't seem to be any trouble this morning.

There were actually more men who'd showed up to work than I'd thought there'd be. I was worried about crossing a picket line, but there was no one picketing at the Central mine. Maybe due to the fact that this was such a small mine, that the miners who wanted to strike were targeting the larger, more productive mines like Standard Shaft in Mount Pleasant, Pennsylvania.

As soon as we got to the first trap door inside the mine, James turned and looked up at me.

"God be with ya, Pa," James said.

"God be with ya, too, son," I replied.

I smiled at my son and swiftly walked through the door that led deep into the mine where I'd be drilling and setting dynamite for the next twelve hours. I was surprised by my son's words. Apparently the boy had paid attention to what many men said to each other upon entering the mine. I suddenly remembered the sound of my own father's voice the last time we had entered a mine together.

"Be safe, and seek God" were the last words my father had said to me. He died that day deep within the Welsh mine, never to be seen again. I was just a young lad then. I'd just driven the mule and wagon out of the mine to unload the coal when the blast occurred. No man was ever recovered. The mine closed that day and became a mass grave for forty souls.

I could still hear the wailing and crying in my dreams. Sometimes I remembered cryin' until my throat was raw. I think of my dear pap being crushed beneath the earth, struggling to breathe while the methane gas burned his eyes and throat. What a most horrendous death. Suffocatin' and bein' crushed to death. Some even drowned if the water level was above their knees. The cave-in pressed their faces to the ground. It was years before my nightmares would end, only to be revived again last night after looking into my young son's eyes after his first day as a coal miner.

Each day passed slowly. Years ago, when Mr. Maurice Painter owned this mine, the men could take a lunch break and go out of the mine for a short time. Mr. Painter was a generous man, but all-too-soon the Central mine was sold to Central Connellsville Coke Company, then to McClure Coke Company. The new owners felt that production was lost to time taken outside of the mine, so the men could no longer see the light of day to eat their lunch. Once they entered the mine, it was there they would stay for the full twelve hours of work, plus the half-hour to eat their lunch by the lights of their carbide lamps.

I was so relieved when the day was finally over that I practically ran out of the shaft where I worked to get to my son at the first door in the mine. James was waiting for me, and when I came into view he ran towards me. At first, I thought James would jump into my arms, like he'd done so many times before when I'd get home from work. But James must have remembered that he was supposed to be a twelve-year-old boy, too big to hug his pa in public. So he put out his little hand and said in as deep a voice as he could muster, "Evenin', Pa."

I got a lump in my throat and wiped my eyes.

"Must have a bit o' coal dust in my eyes," I said

"I did real good today, Pa," James replied.

"Good," I said.

I shortened my stride so James could walk alongside me. We walked in silence until we were crossing the field that led to our house. Once we were sure that no one would hear our conversation, we began to tell each other what the day had been like for each of us.

I realized that God had indeed been with me and my boy today. There had been no problems in the mine, no one caused any arguments, and we were safely walking in the cool breeze of the evening towards home. Although James looked tired, at least he didn't have the look of fear in his young eyes that I'd seen yesterday.

When we got closer to the house we could smell homemade bread. I hadn't realized just how hungry I was until that very moment. James and I looked at each other and then we both began to run for the house. We were both laughing as we ran up the back porch steps.

Anna was just coming out of the kitchen with a pan of hot water for us to wash up. I knew we still would have words when we had some time alone, but for now I was so happy to hear my wife's laughter.

"You both look a sight! Did ya leave any coal dust in the mine today?" Anna asked.

"Yep, Mum, we sure did. That bread sure does smell good," James replied.

"Wash those hands good and get ya inside. Colleen made mulligan stew to go along with the bread," Anna said.

I lost some of my jovial demeanor upon hearing that the O'Malleys were still here. But, then again, I hadn't actually thought that they'd find another place to go to this soon. As I washed my hands and face, I said a silent prayer for God to lead me in how to handle this situation with Peter O'Malley.

When I walked into the kitchen I realized that I wouldn't have to deal with Peter. Just Colleen and her two small children were there.

"Evenin', Colleen," I said.

"Good evenin', William! Peter hasn't returned from job hunting, so Anna was kind enough to let us stay on here. I hope ya don't mind?" Colleen replied.

What could I say? I still considered the O'Malleys our friends, yet I didn't want any trouble for my own family. However, seein' the sadness in Colleen's eyes gave me pause before I answered her.

"We'll do all we can for ya, Colleen. God willin' Peter will find work quickly," I said.

"I appreciate your kindness, William," Colleen said.

CHAPTER EIGHT

PETER O'MALLEY

Saturday – April 4, 1891 – Betrayal

I left early yesterday morning so I wouldn't have to answer any questions. How could I answer Colleen's question when I didn't have the answers myself? I had no idea if I could actually get work in Connellsville. I'd spent the past several months planning a miner's strike with the hopes that it would better the lives of all my friends and co-workers, only to see men senselessly being killed in the streets. And for what? For wanting safer working conditions! For needing real money instead of numbers written on a worthless piece of paper called "script"! For an end to the slavery of working twelve hours in the bowels of the earth and never seeing the light of day!

Colleen and the children would never forgive me. It was bad enough that I'd brought my wife here from Ireland with nothin' but the clothes on our backs, but now we didn't have a roof over our heads. Once the coal police throw ya out there's no gettin' back in the mine.

I'd walked from Rocktown to Tarrs, to jump a train headed towards Connellsville. It wasn't much more than a mile to the main road in Tarrs, where the rails branched off to come to the Central mine. Just as I was nearing the train tracks I heard my oldest son calling out to me.

"Pa, wait for me!" he cried.

"What are ya doin' here, Patrick?" I asked.

"I want to come with ya. James is workin' with his pa now, so I'll work, too," Patrick replied.

"Ya just git on back home! I don't know where I'll end up findin' work, and ya will just hold me up," I shouted.

"But, Pa . . ."

Just then the freight train rounded the bend, slowly pulling the coal cars loaded down with coke. I began to run alongside the train and then I reached up and grabbed hold of the ladder on the nearest coal car, swiftly swinging myself up. Before climbing the ladder I looked back at Patrick, who was still standing beside the railroad tracks. I saw anger in his eyes, but there was something else I read on his face: betrayal.

I watched my son grow smaller as the train swayed along the railroad tracks towards the next coal patch town. I'd have to hide atop the coal until the train reached the town of Connellsville. It was the best possible place for me to find a job.

Connellsville sits on top of a belt of coal with river access to Pittsburgh's steel mills. This town is the hub for all of the surrounding coal patch towns. It includes rail yards, shops, a roundhouse, bridges that cross the Youghiogheny River, and a passenger station.

In South Connellsville, the railroad maintained a stockyard, which had one-hundred pens for cattle, sheep, and pigs. The animals were fed and watered here before being shipped farther east. I figured if I couldn't secure employment in the mines, I'd try the railroad or the stockyards.

From Tarrs to Connellsville is only about ten miles by way of the train, but there were many coal patch towns along the way, and at each town more coal cars were hooked to the engine.

I watched each time the rail workers hooked on more coal cars. I also paid attention to the switch operator when it was time to move the train to a different set of railroad tracks. If I had to, I'd be able to do that job.

When the train was within sight of the town of Connellsville, I climbed down the ladder and dropped to the ground alongside the railroad tracks, being careful to keep my body far from the big steel wheels of the train. I'd walk the rest of the way into town and find the railroad office. It wasn't hard to figure out where to go: There were many people and wagons going to and from the railroad station.

The Connellsville coke industry produced sixty percent of the nation's coke and the product was shipped around the world. Henry Clay Frick owned about half of the coke ovens and, in partnership with Andrew Carnegie, they dominated the steel industry.

The river acted as a natural highway to ship the coke to downriver ports, to iron and steel centers such as Pittsburgh and even Cincinnati, Ohio. If need be, I'd get a job workin' on a barge.

When I found the office of the railroad, I looked down at my worn and dirty clothes. I didn't go in, but walked to the river to wash the coal dirt from my face and hands. My hands were calloused and stained with the sulfur from the mine. There was no hiding the fact that I was a coal miner, but I was determined to turn my life around and to become a railroad man.

Please, God! Let me find work here in this place, I prayed.

As quickly as I'd said the prayer, I was sorry for askin' anything of God. I'd lied to my family and I'd even turned on my best friend, William Millward. No, I'd do no more talkin' to God. From now on, I was on my own. If I got work, I'd send for Colleen and the children, but no more friendships.

I didn't want to have to feel guilty for doin' what I thought was best for me and my family.

I walked into the railroad office and walked up to the first desk I saw. A skinny, balding man with wire spectacles riding down his crooked nose sat behind a large, open ledger.

"Excuse me," I said. "I said, excuse me!" I said once more, in order to get his attention.

"Have an appointment?" he asked.

"No, sir, I don't. I'm in need of a job, and I can do most anythin' ya got," I said.

The man took off his spectacles and looked up at me through squinting eyes. He didn't seem like the type of man who'd work for a railroad. He looked me up and down and his gaze rested on my hands instead of my face.

"Looks like ya be a workin' man. Where ya from, lad?" he asked.

"I'm from Ireland. I have a wife and three children to support and I need to find work at once," I replied.

"So, ya ever worked for the railroad before?" he asked.

"No, sir, but I'm willin' to do whatever it takes. I'm strong and I can start work today. Do ya have any work?" I asked.

The man stood up and I was surprised to see that he wasn't much taller than my son Patrick. His hands looked as soft as a child's hands, and he didn't show much emotion on his homely face. However, he did extend his hand to me.

"Wait here 'til I speak with Mr. Jones. Don't know if he can use another man on the trains, but could be he could use a rail yard worker. My name's Peabody. Forrest Peabody. Ya can call me Forrest," he said as he scurried to the back of the office building and disappeared through a large set of doors.

I didn't know who this Mr. Jones was, nor did I care. Just as long as he could give me a job and a room to sleep in until I could find a place for my family. I didn't have any money and I hadn't thought to ask Anna Millward to pack a lunch for me. I was hoping that I could help someone on the loading dock for a bit of food or a few pennies.

It wasn't long before Mr. Peabody came back to his desk. He motioned for me to take a seat across the room, near a small writing table. After shuffling through some papers, he found what he was lookin' for and looked up at me.

"Can ya read 'n write?" he asked.

"Some," I replied.

"Write down your name and where you'll be a-stayin'," he replied.

"I just got into town, and I don't have a place to stay yet. Could ya give me an idea of where I can sleep for the night?" I asked.

"No one gives strangers credit in this town, but if you'll be willin' to work a few hours without pay, ya can see ol' Mr. Murphy over at the tavern. He's been known to help out the Irishmen who wander in. Got a cot in his back storeroom; nothin' fancy but it'll do 'til ya make a few cents," Mr. Peabody replied.

"Thank ya for that," I said as I took the paper and pencil from Mr. Peabody.

I leaned over the desk and wrote my name and the names of my family members. I didn't want to call attention to the fact that I'd been involved with the miner's strike, so I listed my address in Ireland, where me and Colleen had come from so long ago.

Mr. Peabody looked at the paper I had handed back to him and raised his eyebrows. He may look meek, but Peabody was no fool. He knew right off that I was hidin' somethin', and it showed on his face.

"Where'd ya live after comin' from Ireland?" Peabody asked.

"Does it matter?" I replied.

"It does if ya have a mind to cause trouble. Mr. Jones don't take kindly to troublemakers," Peabody said.

"You'll get no trouble from me, Mr. Peabody. I just want to work and bring my family to this town. As I told ya, I'm a hard worker and I'll do most anythin' to earn an honest pay. Now, can ya tell me where I might seek a place for my wife and three young'uns?" I asked.

"There be a few empty shacks down by the railroad tracks, just past the bridge on Crawford Avenue. Don't know for sure who owns 'em, but ya can ask around. Bein' that it's spring, maybe ya can make due until ya find a better house. I'll go in and talk with Mr. Jones and see if he has need of ya," Peabody replied.

It seemed like a long time before Peabody came out of the office of Mr. Jones. I was beginning to worry about what was being said behind the closed doors when suddenly the biggest man I had ever seen came through the doors, ducking his head to clear the seven-foot-tall arch. Peabody was scurrying behind him like a frightened mouse.

"You be Peter O'Malley?" Mr. Jones asked.

"Yes, sir!" I answered as I put my right hand towards Jones.

"I understand ya can start work today. I need a strong man to help at the roundhouse. We've got an engine down and repairs must be made quickly. Are ya quick on your feet?" Jones asked.

"Yes, sir! I'll do any job ya have, and I'll make ya proud," I replied.

"Peabody said ya have a family. I'd be willin' to advance ya pay on a daily basis so ya can get food and such for 'em. Now, that's only if ya do an honest day's work. If ya can't do the work, ya get no pay. Understand?" Mr. Jones said.

Only then did Mr. Jones extend his hand to me. He, too, could see that I was hiding something. By hiring me on a day-to-day basis, there wouldn't be any reason to terminate the working relationship if he found out that I was, indeed, a troublemaker.

After shaking hands, we parted ways. Mr. Jones went back into his office and I ran to the roundhouse to begin my new job. I'd have to work for a week or so to get enough money to hire a wagon to fetch Colleen, the children, and our meager belongings from Rocktown to Connellsville. It never occurred to me that this plan would not be acceptable to my wife. Didn't matter, anyway; she'd do as she was told.

CHAPTER NINE

COLLEEN O'MALLEY

Saturday – April 4, 1891 – Broken

For the past two days I've been living a nightmare. On April 2 Peter went to the Morewood mine to protest against working conditions of the coal company. In all, nine men were killed, making this day the Morewood Massacre.

The coal police and some Pinkerton agents went from house to house, evicting anyone who had taken part in the march on Morewood Street. Had it not been for Gretchen Klink and Anna Millward, I don't know what I would have done. I watched in shock as all of my personal belongings were thrown out into the street.

Peter not only lost his job but our home, as well. I thought that the coal police were going to kill Peter when they threw him to the ground in front of our house. However, I was so mad at him that I wanted to kill him myself.

The gentle Irishman I'd married was gone. Over the past several years Peter had begun to resent the mine owners. He began going to the tavern after work several evenings a week and urging the men to strike. At first, the local men would have a few pints with him and then go home. But then there were miners from the surrounding towns who had come to join in the meetings.

When a neighbor told me that Peter had called William Millward a scab, and that Patrick was picking fights at school as well, I was more than ashamed. I was humiliated. These people had been our friends for nearly eleven years. We were all immigrants, just trying to make a living.

I wasn't even upset when Peter left yesterday morning. We'd barely discussed his going to Connellsville to see if he could get a job with the railroad; however, we needed some time apart. The children and I were staying with William and Anna Millward, but they couldn't keep us much longer. The tension of Peter and William being in the same house was unbearable. Luckily, they weren't together for very long. Peter got out of bed long before daylight and left without so much as a goodbye.

When Patrick left right after Peter yesterday morning, I didn't worry much about him. I figured he'd talk with his pa and then go on to school. It wasn't until dinner time that I began to get worried. When William and James got home from the mine, James offered to go around to each house and ask if anyone had seen Patrick. Benjamin told us that Patrick had not been in school, either.

Anna insisted that we stay another night with them, for which I was grateful. After all, where else could I go with two small children and one missing nine-year-old? I was only praying that William wouldn't have any problems at the mine because of us staying here. Everyone was under scrutiny if they associated with troublemakers.

Once I got Michael and Adel to fall asleep, I went outside, to sit under the grape arbor. It had been such a long time since I had prayed.

"Dear Lord, please be with my family. I feel like we're falling apart, and I don't know what to do! Please bring my son home and change the heart of Peter. Give him a good job and help him to once

more be a good husband and father. Forgive me, Lord, for being so far from you for so long. I pray to You in Jesus's name. Amen."

The wind began to pick up and clouds drifted over the crescent moon. Suddenly I felt a dark and sinister presence surrounding my very soul. Call it "mother's intuition," or just plain fear, but I began to shake uncontrollably. Just then I saw a man walking up to the Millwards' front door. Within minutes Anna came running out to the grape arbor, followed by William and the stranger.

"What is it, Anna?" I cried.

"Colleen, a boy was found along the railroad tracks near Old Bethany yesterday. He hasn't been identified, but he was taken to a doctor's office in Scottdale," Anna exclaimed.

This couldn't be happening. My son must be with his father.

"Oh, dear God! Please, not my son," I cried.

The stranger stepped forward and introduced himself as Joseph Gettemy. He was a resident of Old Bethany who worked on the railroad.

"I can take you to see the child," Joseph said.

"Go with him, Colleen. I'll tend to your little ones," Anna replied.

"I haven't any money to pay you, Mr. Gettemy," I cried.

"No need for pay. I just hope we can find the child's parents," Joseph stated.

I ran to the waiting wagon that Mr. Gettemy had driven from Scottdale. The old mule pulling the wagon looked tired and worn out from working in the coal mine, but I was thankful that we wouldn't have to walk the four miles to the doctor's home.

As the mule pulled us up the hill towards the Tarrs church, I turned to look at Mr. Gettemy. He had a kind face, and apparently a kind heart as well. Why else would he take the time to try and find a child's parents when he'd worked a long day in the mine with his mule?

"Mr. Gettemy, did you talk with my son?" I asked.

"Don't rightly know if the boy is actually your son, but he's in no shape for talkin'. I think it's best if ya see 'im before learnin' too much right now. Might not be your boy," Joseph replied.

"How old would you say this child is, Mr. Gettemy?" I asked.

"Don't have no children of my own, so I don't rightly know. Doc says he's 'bout eight or nine years old," Joseph said.

"His hair. What color is his hair?" I cried.

"Don't know! It was evenin' when I heard 'bout the child. A freight train stopped and picked him up and then took him to Scottdale in the caboose. When I got done with my shift the whole town was abuzz 'bout the accident. The men who had children went to take a look at him, but no one knows who the child belongs to. Since he was found along the railroad tracks near Old Bethany people started askin' around, and one of the miner's wives said she'd heard a rumor that a child from Rocktown was lost. Then we heard 'bout Millward takin' in a family who'd been evicted, so I said I'd come to talk with Millward. I can't tell ya much else," Joseph replied.

We rode the rest of the way to Scottdale in silence. We pulled up to a large, Victorian home with a sign that read *Doctor Martin Gilbert* hanging from a post out front. The house was dark, but as soon as I ran up the wooden steps the front door opened.

"Doctor, I'm Colleen O'Malley. I've come to see if the child you're tendin' is my son!" I cried.

"Come in! Before I take you back to see him, I want to prepare you, Mrs. O'Malley. Even if it isn't your boy, it will be hard for any woman to see a child in such bad shape," Dr. Gilbert replied.

"Please, just let me see him at once!" I cried.

I followed the doctor through the front room, to an examining room in the center of the big house. Behind a curtain was a small bed and a table with a lamp on it. The soft lighting made it hard to see the child's face. However, his bright-red hair told me who this child was. I knew without a doubt that this was my son. My Patrick!

I ran to his side and gently touched his face. He was so hot, yet his face was ashen in color.

"Patrick, it's Ma. Please wake up now, son!" I cried.

"Mrs. O'Malley, your son is in very bad shape. He's lost his right leg and his left foot is crushed. I've tried to keep him stable, but I'll have to amputate the foot in the morning. I'm afraid that infection has set in and his fever is just too high for me to do any more tonight," Dr. Gilbert replied.

I began to shake all over. How could this have happened? Where was Peter?

"Doctor, can you tell me what happened to my son?" I asked.

"It looks like he was attempting to jump on a train and he must have fallen beneath the wheels. By the time he was seen by the caboose conductor, he'd lost quite a lot of blood. His right leg was completely severed, so all the man could do was wrap the wound tightly. It was the second train that came through that stopped to pick up the child, and then he got him to me as quickly as possible," Dr. Gilbert replied.

"Will he live?" I cried.

"Mrs. O'Malley, I'd like you to stay near the child for the night. Would you like me to get you a cup of coffee or tea?" Dr. Gilbert asked.

"No, I need nothin'," I replied.

"Just call out if you see any change in the child. By the way, what is his name?" Dr. Gilbert asked.

"His name is Patrick."

Dr. Gilbert turned the kerosene lantern to low and turned to leave the room. He stopped and looked back at me with such empathy in his eyes.

"Mrs. O'Malley, my wife will look in on you in a while. Don't hesitate to ask for anything. I'm sure it will be a long night for you," Dr. Gilbert replied.

I sat on the small wooden chair beside the bed, holding my son's hand. Although his head was hot with fever, his tiny hand was cold and clammy. He was barely breathing. I lifted the white sheet covering his little body and saw only bandages where his precious leg used to be. Blood seeped through the bandages of his left foot.

Should I call out to the doctor? I wondered. I fell to my knees beside the bed and lowered my head to rest on my son's thin chest. His heartbeat was so weak. I wondered how long he had been lying on the tracks, afraid and alone. His pain must have been terrible. Did he call out for his pa? Was Peter even near when this happened? I had so many unanswered questions. Nothing made any sense anymore.

I was just beginning to get drowsy when I heard footsteps.

"Mrs. O'Malley, I've brought you a cup of tea," Mrs. Gilbert said.

"Thank you!" I replied.

Doctor Gilbert came into the room, behind his wife. He looked as though he hadn't slept at all in the past two days. As I reached out to take the cup from Mrs. Gilbert, the doctor began to examine Patrick.

"Mrs. O'Malley, would you like to take your tea to the sitting room where you can stretch your legs a bit?" Mrs. Gilbert asked.

"I'd like to stay close to my son if you don't mind," I replied.

The doctor and Mrs. Gilbert exchanged worried glances as he proceeded to attend to Patrick. I watched as the doctor put a stethoscope to Patrick's chest, and then he put his fingers on Patrick's neck. Mrs. Gilbert came swiftly to my side as her husband shook his head from side to side.

"NO!" I screamed.

The beautiful, rose-patterned china cup fell to the floor and smashed into pieces. There was a roaring in my head as I, too, fell to the floor. Losing consciousness was a blessing.

CHAPTER TEN

ANNA MILLWARD

Sunday – April 5, 1891 – A Time of Mourning

Colleen's little ones didn't sleep well last night, so I gave up any idea of goin' to church this mornin'. Adel has been weaned for several months now, but she's cried for her mama and sucked her thumb non-stop ever since Colleen left for Scottdale yesterday.

Michael knew something was very wrong, since his pa had left without telling the little guy goodbye, and his mama had been so upset while she was here. When she left with a strange man yesterday he didn't cry, but his tears came at bedtime. Benjamin and Jacob did their best to try and keep him busy. They even slept with him on the bed of quilts I'd made for them on the floor.

I was just washing the breakfast dishes when a large buckboard wagon, pulled by a mule, drove up to our house. I recognized from the night before the man who was knocking on our front door. I called out to William to go and see what he wanted.

"Anna, ya best come into the livin' room," William said after he'd let Mr. Gettemy in.

"Mornin', Mrs. Millward. I've come to talk with you about Colleen O'Malley," Mr. Gettemy said.

"What's happened to Colleen?" I asked.

"She needs ya to come with me to Scottdale right away. Her son is dead, and he's being buried this afternoon in St. John's Cemetery. Colleen has asked me to fetch you and her young'uns. I'm also gonna take her belongings to a small shack her husband's rented in Connellsville," Mr. Gettemy replied.

"Oh, no! What happened to Patrick?" I cried.

"He was run over by a train two days ago. He lost so much blood that the doctor couldn't save him. He died yesterday mornin'. Took us most of yesterday to find his pa. Seems he started a new job in Connellsville, workin' for the railroad. I offered to help 'em out, but I can't take two small children in the wagon by myself," Mr. Gettemy explained.

"Anna, ya shouldn't be travelin' in your condition. Let me fetch Gretchen Klink to go with Mr. Gettemy and the O'Malley children," William said.

"I'll be fine, William. I've got almost a whole month before the baby is due, and Colleen needs me right now. Sarah can take care of our little ones. Mr. Gettemy, can you bring me back home tonight?" I asked.

"Yes, I'll bring ya back just as soon as I git back from Connellsville. I'll have to wait until the funeral is over so I can take Mrs. O'Malley and her children to her husband. We should be back in Rocktown before dark," Mr. Gettemy replied.

"Mr. Gettemy, can ya pull the wagon to the shed out back? I'll help ya load the O'Malleys' things," William said.

"Please, call me Joe. I appreciate ya helpin'," Mr. Gettemy said.

As the men went to load the wagon, I called my three oldest children into the kitchen. I didn't want them to hear this horrible news at school tomorrow. Bad news always travels fast, and I knew everyone was talking about the child that had been hit by a train. Until now, we didn't know who that child was. James and Patrick had played together since they were born. I was sure this news would be hard for my children to comprehend.

"What's wrong, Mum?" James, Benjamin, and Sarah all asked at the same time.

"Sarah, would ya please get Adel and Michael dressed for me? Your pa will explain to ya what has happened after I take the children to their mother," I said.

"Yes, Mum," Sarah said.

Once Sarah had gone into the bedroom to dress the O'Malley children, I pulled my two oldest boys close and hugged them.

"The child that was hit by the train on Friday was Patrick O'Malley. He died yesterday. Colleen needs me to take her children to Scottdale, where Patrick will be buried. I want ya all to be good. Boys, ya mind Sarah. She's gonna help Pa while I'm gone," I replied.

Jacob and Delilah were playing with Michael and Adel in the bedroom. I didn't want to tell them anything just yet. They were all so young, and I didn't think I should be the one to tell Michael and Adel that their big brother was dead.

"When are ya comin' back home?" James asked.

"I'll be back tonight," I said.

"Ma, can't I go with ya?" James asked.

"No, your pa will need ya to help him and Sarah with the young'uns today. Besides, you need your rest after workin' so many hours in the mine this week," I said.

James turned and went straight to his bedroom. I could tell that he was very upset, but I didn't want him to go to the funeral. It would be very hard on Colleen, and I had no idea if Peter would be there or not. I'm sure losing a child in such a way was a shock, and I had so many questions as to how and why this had happened. I wanted to spare my son the pain of seeing the O'Malley family at this tumultuous time.

I put a loaf of bread, a jar of jelly, and a butcher's knife into a basket and placed a dish towel over the top. I didn't know if Colleen's children would get hungry during the ride from Rocktown to Scottdale. It shouldn't take very long to get there. Whatever wasn't eaten today I'd give to Colleen to take home.

It didn't take William and Mr. Gettemy long to load the wagon. I was coming out of the back door as Mr. Gettemy was climbing up onto the driver's seat of the wagon. He clicked the reins and the old mule's ears stood up as he began pulling the wagon across the lawn.

"Let me git the wagon on the street before ya climb on, Mrs. Millward. It'll be less bumpy for ya there," Mr. Gettemy said.

"Sarah, please bring Adel and Michael outside," I loudly called out.

It was nice to know that Mr. Gettemy was looking out for my comfort, as well as doing so much for Colleen and her family. William helped me up into the wagon and then he handed Adel and Michael up to me.

"Please be careful, Anna," William whispered as his lips brushed my cheek.

"Don't worry 'bout me, William. I'll take care," I replied.

Once I was settled on the bench seat beside Mr. Gettemy, he clicked the reins as he said, "Easy now, Jake."

The old mule acted like he understood what his owner was saying. He walked slow and steady, pulling the loaded wagon with ease. Mr. Gettemy barely had to touch the reins as the mule followed the road from whence they had come.

"Where we goin', Mrs. Millward?" Michael asked.

"Your mama is in a town called Scottdale, and she asked me to bring you and Adel to her," I answered as enthusiastically as I could.

"How long 'til we git there?" Michael asked.

"We'll be there in time for lunch, young man. Would ya like to help me drive the mule?" Mr. Gettemy replied.

"Sure! How do ya drive a mule?" Michael said as he climbed up on Mr. Gettemy's lap.

"Ya just hold on to the reins, and when we have to go left or right, I'll show ya what to do. Mule's name is Jake. Just call out to 'im: *Git up, Jake!*" Mr. Gettemy said.

"Git up, Jake!" Michael called out, and the mule picked up his step at once. At this pace we'd be in Scottdale in no time at all.

Adel sat on my lap, leaning against my breast, suckin' her thumb. I'd never noticed that she was a thumb-sucker before. I guess the stress of the past several days made even the children nervous. I rubbed her tiny back and she was soon fast asleep.

We rode in silence for several miles. Michael was holdin' onto the reins so tightly that his little knuckles were white. When we got to Old Bethany, there was a long, steep hill with several turns along the way, so Mr. Gettemy put his hands in front of Michael's to steer the mule. The distraction of helpin' to drive the mule made Michael smile. Soon he was talkin' up a storm with Mr. Gettemy, askin' all kinds of question about Jake the mule.

I found comfort in holdin' Colleen's little girl. It gave me someone to hold on to. I was so worried about my friend and her family. Mr. Gettemy hadn't mentioned Peter O'Malley. I had no idea where Colleen had spent the night, or where Peter was. I feared that Colleen had had to face the death of her son alone.

It took a couple of hours to get from Rocktown to Scottdale with the load on the wagon. Just as we were pullin' up to the doctor's house, on Chestnut Street, another wagon approached from the opposite direction. Before it was at a complete stop, Peter O'Malley jumped down from the wagon and ran toward the front door.

As he pounded on the door, Adel awoke and began to cry. Then Michael shouted, "Pa, I'm over here! Pa, come git me."

The doctor opened the door and asked Peter to come in, closing the door at once. Both children began to cry uncontrollably. I tried to quiet them, but all they understood was that their parents had been gone for several days and now their pa didn't stop to talk with them.

"Mrs. Millward, I'll git down with the boy, and then help you and the little one down," Mr. Gettemy said.

"Thank you! If ya don't mind, I'd like to see what's goin' on in the doctor's office before I take the children in. Can ya please keep them outside for just a while longer?" I asked.

"Yep, be glad to help. Come on, Michael, and help me water ol' Jake," Mr. Gettemy said as he took Adel from my arms then reached for Michael's hand.

I hurried up the path to the doctor's house, and the door opened before I could raise my hand to knock. A woman with gray hair and a sympathetic smile stepped aside so I could enter the front room. I could hear voices comin' from a room near the back of the house.

"Could ya please tell me if Colleen O'Malley is here?" I asked.

"She is in a spare bedroom just across the hall from my husband's examining room. Are you family?" the woman asked.

"No, I'm her best friend, Anna Millward. I've been keepin' her children, and she sent word for me to bring them to her along with all of her belongings. How is she doin'?" I asked.

"I'm Dr. Gilbert's wife, Estelle. I've been tending to Mrs. O'Malley since her son passed. She's very upset, as any mother would be, but she's also very angry. Her husband has just now come. Their child is to be buried this afternoon. Perhaps you could go in with them to offer your support. I'm sure they would appreciate seeing a friend about now," Mrs. Gilbert whispered.

"Yes, I'm sure that Colleen needs me, but do you think I should give them a few more minutes alone?" I asked.

"No! If you don't mind, I think you should go to her now. I don't mean to sound harsh, but she told me that she didn't even want to see her husband. She's blaming him for this accident and I just don't know what she's planning to do after the funeral. Please go to her, " Mrs. Gilbert replied.

I walked to the door of the bedroom, listening for the right moment to open it. Just as I was turning the doorknob, I heard a sharp slap, and then Peter pushed past me and ran outside.

I ran to Colleen's side and she collapsed in my arms. Her sobs were like that of a wounded animal. She shook with each breath, and her tears dampened my shoulders. I couldn't control myself a moment more—I began to cry, too. We stood like that for what seemed like a very long time. Just holdin' on to each other and sobbin' until Mrs. Gilbert quietly entered the room.

"Mrs. O'Malley, the undertaker is here. He asked if you and your husband would like to ride behind the horse-drawn funeral wagon. Mr. Gettemy has offered to take you and your family to the church and then to the cemetery in his wagon," Mrs. Gilbert said.

"I don't want to go anywhere with that man ever again!" Colleen screamed.

"Now, Colleen, you don't mean that. Your children need you to be strong for them, and Peter needs you, too," I replied.

"Where was he when my boy was hurt? Where was he when Patrick died? I don't want to talk to him. Not today, not ever!" Colleen cried.

I put my arm around Colleen's shoulders and led her out of the doctor's house. Mr. Gettemy was unloading all of the O'Malleys' belongings from his wagon and onto the wagon that Peter had brought from Connellsville.

An elderly gentleman with long, white hair sat on the wagon seat, holdin' the reins of the biggest team of workhorses that I'd ever seen. Peter was quietly talkin' to the man, no doubt givin' him instructions on when he'd be ready to return to Connellsville. He held a child on each knee, and he was rubbin' their little backs with his big, calloused hands.

Mr. Gettemy had just put the last of the O'Malleys' belongings on the wagon; he came over to me and Colleen.

"May I help you ladies up on the wagon?" Mr. Gettemy asked.

"Thank ya, Mr. Gettemy," I replied.

Colleen didn't say a word. She just reached for the step on the front of the wagon and pulled herself up. Mr. Gettemy helped me up, climbed onto the wagon with ease, and clicked to ol' Jake.

Peter and the children followed close behind us in the old man's wagon. It was a sad procession; the funeral wagon, the old buckboard, and a livery wagon. There were no other friends, no one to have a wake for Patrick, and no flowers to place upon the plain, wooden casket.

When we got to St. John's Church, the priest came out to greet the family of Patrick O'Malley. Peter and Mr. Gettemy carried the small casket into the church and placed it on the floor, in front of the altar.

I'd never been in a Catholic church before and I was surprised at how beautiful it was. Colleen had told me a lot about her religion, but I never expected to see life-sized statues of Jesus and Mary. They were so realistic and so awe-inspiring. I led the children to the first pew in the front of the church. Colleen sat next to Michael, and when Peter came into the church he sat on the other side of Michael.

The ol' man with white hair and Mr. Gettemy sat in the back of the church. I guess they didn't want to intrude on the grieving family, or maybe they weren't Catholic. Whatever the case, I was glad that they came to offer their condolences to Colleen and Peter.

Colleen stared straight ahead, refusing to look at Peter. The service was long, and spoken entirely in Latin. I didn't understand what was goin' on, but it was spoken so eloquently by the young priest that I felt close to God just being in this place.

When the priest was done talkin', he sang a song and then motioned for the casket to be taken out to the wagon. The drive down Broadway from St. John's Church to the cemetery didn't take very long. Two young men were standing near the grave that they had just finished diggin', and the priest walked behind the men who were carrying the casket. As they lowered the casket into the grave, I heard Colleen and Peter crying. I stood back from the grave about ten feet, holding Adel and Michael close to my side. They, too, were crying softly. I wasn't sure if either of them understood that their big brother was in that pine box, but they knew their parents were sad, and that made them sad as well.

As soon as the funeral was over, the priest walked back to his church and I took the children to Mr. Gettemy's wagon. He helped us all up into the wagon, where we sat on burlap sacks and I made us all jelly sandwiches.

Colleen and Peter stayed by the grave talking for a long time, and when they finally came over to the wagon, neither one said a word. Peter reached up and took Michael in his arms, and Colleen took Adel, and then she turned to walk to the old man's wagon.

"Colleen, where are ya goin'?" I asked.

"I'll go with Peter to Connellsville to live, but I'll never consider him my husband again. I'll live with him until our children are raised because I've nowhere else to go. Goodbye, Anna."

"Will ya write me with your address, Colleen?" I cried.

"Don't think I'll be able to, Anna. We've nothin' in common now," Colleen replied.

Mr. Gettemy pulled his wagon around to head back towards Rocktown. He got down from his seat and helped me onto the seat beside him. We rode the whole way to my home in silence. Neither of us felt like talkin' after watchin' this once-happy family fall apart.

William came outside as soon as he heard the clip-clop of the mule's feet comin' up the road. The children all ran out of the house behind him. When Mr. Gettemy stopped the wagon, William reached up and lifted me down. I thanked Mr. Gettemy for all that he'd done for me and for the O'Malleys.

As soon as I walked into my little kitchen, I sat down on a chair and began to cry. All of my children gathered 'round me, rubbin' my back and tellin' me that they loved me. William came in after sayin' his goodbyes to Mr. Gettemy. He and Sarah got supper on the table and then the older children helped the little ones get ready for bed. William said the nightly prayers with the children and tucked them all in. When we finally got into our own bed, I told William of all that had happened, and we held each other and cried.

CHAPTER ELEVEN

GRETCHEN KLINK

Wednesday – April 8, 1891 – A New Life

It isn't uncommon for someone to be knockin' on my door in the middle of the night. After all, I am a midwife, and I was expectin' to hear from the Millward family. Anna was due to have her sixth child anytime now. In fact, I thought she'd deliver this baby early, since she had gone ridin' all over the countryside in a wagon.

I pulled on my bathrobe and hurried to the kitchen door. Just as I expected: It was the oldest Millward boy, James.

"Miss Klink, Mum says for ya to come quick. It's time for the baby to be born. My pa didn't want to leave her 'cause he said this one might come before ya can walk to our house," James yelled breathlessly.

"James, calm down. I'll pull on a dress and git my bag. It won't take but a minute and we'll be out the door," I replied.

True to my word, we were quickly on our way. I always keep a dress and my birthin' bag hangin' on a nail behind my bedroom door. Babies wait for no one, so I've learned to always be prepared. James ran ahead of me into the darkness, and then he turned around and ran back to me, shinin' the lantern he carried in his right hand.

"Sorry, Miss Klink! Pa said to hold the lantern for ya. I didn't mean to run ahead of ya," James said.

"I'm doin' just fine. There's a full moon tonight to light my way and besides I've walked to your house enough times that I could walk the path in my sleep. Are ya excited to git another brother or sister?" I asked.

"I hope it's a boy, but I wouldn't say that I'm excited 'bout havin' another mouth to feed," James replied.

I knew that James was now working in the mine with his father, so I could understand why he didn't care to have another child in the family. I'd delivered many babies in this little coal patch town and it sometimes baffled me as to why they just kept having children when they could barely feed themselves.

Of course, it was different for me, since I'd never married. When my brother was killed in the mine I continued to be the housekeeper to Maurice Painter and his son Jake. It was Mr. Painter that brought it to my attention that my brother Hans had cheated me out of quite a lot of money.

Hans had insisted that Mr. Painter pay him each month for the work that I did in the Painter household. Mr. Painter told me to get all of their food and supplies at the company store on his account. Since he was the owner of the mine I just had to tell the storekeeper what was needed, and no money ever exchanged hands. I didn't realize that my brother would be so devious as to keep my pay. Hans told me that the house we lived in was paid for by my services to the Painters.

I was sure I'd be evicted from our house when Hans died, but Mr. Painter asked me to stay on as his housekeeper. I'd looked everywhere for the money that Hans had swindled from me, but didn't find it until a year after his death. I was cleaning out a dresser drawer when I accidentally dropped the drawer on the floor and a false bottom fell out of it. There were documents from when we came from Germany, plus several thousands of dollars wrapped in an old rag. Hans had gone to a lot of trouble to keep his stash a secret. If I hadn't dropped that drawer I never would have found the money.

I was very fond of Jake and I was falling in love with Maurice. Everyone in the patch thought that Maurice would propose to me because we were always together. Although, we had never spent the night together—Maurice was always mindful of my reputation. We went together to many of the social events in the little community of Central, but I had never made love to Maurice.

However, Maurice Painter eventually sold the mine to the McClure Coal and Coke Company and he and Jake moved to another town. He told me about his plans only one week before they moved, and he also told me that the house had been deeded to me, so I was free and clear of any financial responsibility to him. As if this would make me happy. Since I'd found the money, I could afford to support myself from that along with any payment I'd receive for being a midwife, but that didn't stop the sting of knowing that I wasn't important to Maurice. I was only his employee after all. I vowed that I would never fall in love again.

All of these memories came back to me as I walked to the Millward home. I had delivered all of Anna's babies over the past nine years so I guess that's why we are so close. Just as I was walking across the Millwards' yard, I saw William open the back door and look outside.

"Gretchen, please hurry. I think the baby is coming now!" William cried.

"Please put a pot of water on the stove to boil, and then ya can take the little ones outside to the swing. Just in case Anna needs to cry out, they won't be afraid for her," I replied.

As I entered the bedroom, Anna was doing her best to keep calm. By the look on her face she was in the middle of a strong contraction. I put on my birthing apron and took out the scissors and clean towels to wash the newborn.

"I'm here, Anna. Let me examine ya to see how far along ya are," I said.

"Oh, I'm so glad you got here. I was so afraid that William would have to help me deliver this one," Anna replied.

"I've sent him and the children outside, so go ahead and scream if the pain gets too bad," I said as I checked to see how close Anna was to giving birth. "It won't be long now. Only a few more good pushes and we'll see if ya have a baby girl or a baby boy."

Anna seemed to be afraid. When the next contraction started, I grabbed hold of Anna's arms and pulled her up, almost into a sitting position. Anna let out one loud scream, and then the baby slipped out of her body. I immediately let go of Anna and lifted the baby up by her feet, giving her one swift smack on the butt.

"Ya have a beautiful little girl, Anna!" I exclaimed.

I put the baby across Anna's stomach and went into the kitchen to get a bowl of hot water to sterilize the scissors before cutting the umbilical cord. When I came back into the room Anna was smiling down at her baby with tears running down her cheeks.

"Are ya doin' all right Anna?" I asked.

"Yes, we're doin' just fine. Except I don't know how we'll afford to feed another young'un once she's weaned," Anna whispered.

"Well, Anna, ya taught me to trust in the Lord for all our needs. Don't ya think He will help ya with one more babe?" I replied.

"Yes, I guess He will. I'm so tired, Gretchen. This baby was much harder to birth than the other five. Do ya think somethin's wrong?" Anna asked.

"No, I just think ya be a bit older now. Have ya thought of a name for this little girl?" I asked as I cut and tied the cord.

Anna watched as I washed her baby and then wrapped her in a clean baby blanket. She really hadn't thought of any girls' names. She and William had both referred to this baby as being a boy.

"We didn't discuss girls' names. Maybe I'll let Sarah name her. She's been such a big help to me these past nine months, I'm sure she'd be so happy to name the baby," Anna replied.

"That's a wonderful idea," I replied as I cleaned Anna up and then took the towels that were beneath her, rolling them up to be burned. Once I had both mother and baby presentable I went to the back door to call in the whole Millward family to meet the new arrival.

As soon as William saw the kitchen door opening, he was on his feet and running across the lawn to go inside. Sarah picked up Delilah and ran closely behind her pa; all of the other children followed behind them.

When William got to the door, he turned around and put his finger to his lips to signal the children to be quiet. As they entered the bedroom, Anna was sitting up in the bed, holding the tightly-wrapped baby in her arms.

"Ma, what is it?" Sarah asked.

"It's a little girl. Children, ya have a new baby sister," Anna replied.

William reached out to take the baby from Anna, then he got down on his knees to let the children get their first look at the baby. He also said a quick prayer to God, thanking Him for this beautiful child and for a safe delivery. So many women were known to die in childbirth in the coal patch towns and William never took the birth of a baby lightly.

"Ma, what are ya gonna name her?" Sarah asked.

"William, if ya don't mind, I was gonna let Sarah name her," Anna replied.

"That's a wonderful idea. Sarah, what name suits a little sister?" William asked.

Sarah gazed at the baby in William's arms for several minutes before she answered.

"Ma, can I hold her? I need to get to know her before just blurtin' out a name. It has to be a pretty name, one that she'll like when she gets older," Sarah replied.

"Come sit in the rockin' chair, Sarah, and hold her real close to ya," William said as he then placed the baby in Sarah's arms.

I watched this tender scene and then turned to go out into the kitchen. Delivering a baby never gets old. There is a special feeling when a child is born healthy and loved, although there are many times when the outcome wasn't as good as this one. Some people don't look at the birth of a child as a blessing. There are so many hard times and never enough money for the coal miners and their families.

William came out into the kitchen to talk with me. They hadn't discussed a fee for delivering the baby. I knew that William and Anna didn't have a lot of money saved, but they also didn't expect me to do this free of charge. I didn't want to embarrass the Millwards by charging more than they could afford.

"Gretchen, what do we owe ya for helpin' Anna have this baby?" William asked.

"I know times are hard for everyone, William. I'd be happy with one of those nice layin' hens ya have in the coop out back and maybe a bit of bacon when ya butcher the in hog in the fall," I replied.

"Now Gretchen, I know ya being kind. I don't expect ya to work for free. Ya be welcome to a chicken and I'm sure Anna was plannin' to give ya some bacon, so please name a price," William said.

"Do ya think a dollar would be too much to ask?" I asked.

"A dollar isn't much of a fee, but I'll be happy to give it," William whispered.

I watched as William went to the cookie jar that sat on the kitchen shelf that was made out of rough lumber. He took out a silver dollar and handed it to me with a smile on his face. I suddenly felt that my fee for delivering this baby was paid in full. I'd done something to make my friends happy. This was what makes my job worthwhile.

I went in to check on Anna and the baby once more before returning home. Anna was nursing the little one, while her oldest daughter watched from the rocking chair.

"Gretchen, thank you so much for coming quickly. Sarah has decided to name the baby Elizabeth," Anna said.

"That's a beautiful name, Sarah. Did you name the baby after a family member or a friend?" I asked.

"I named her after Jesus's aunt. I remembered a story from the Bible about Jesus's mother going to visit her cousin, Elizabeth. They were both gonna have a baby. Elizabeth named her baby John and Mary named her baby Jesus, just like the angel of the Lord told her to do. I figured that Elizabeth is a good Christian name. Don't you agree, Miss Klink?" Sarah asked.

"Yes, that's a fine name," I replied.

"Do ya need anything before I leave, Anna?" I asked.

"No, I'm sure that Sarah will be able to tend to the children, and I have a big pot of soup that I made yesterday so dinner will be easy to get ready. Would ya like a jar of soup to take home for dinner, Gretchen?" Anna asked.

"No, but thank ya for offerin'. I'll stop by tomorrow to check on ya. If ya have any problems just send someone to fetch me. Stay in bed today and rest," I said as I turned to go.

CHILDHOOD LOST

PART TWO

CHAPTER TWELVE

JAMES D. MILLWARD

January 26, 1904 – Dangerous Times

As I was walkin' to the mine I was thinkin' of the dream I kept havin' for the past week. It was the same dream over and over again: I was nine years old and I'd just started workin' in the Central mine. That old fear of darkness made me awaken with sweat pourin' down my face. I hadn't thought of my first mine job in a very long time. I couldn't figure out why I was frettin' 'bout it now. I was only a "nipper" for a year. Although I didn't like sittin' alone in the darkness, I knew I had to do my share to help out our family.

When I turned ten years old I began drivin' a mule, then at twelve I began loadin' the wagons with coal after my pa did the blastin'. It was hard work, but it was better than sittin' alone all day in the dark. At least there were other men to talk to, and the busier I kept the faster the day went.

Maybe I was havin' these dreams because of a young Hungarian boy named Miklos who was crushed last week. My pa warned me right on that I had to be quick 'bout openin' the trap door for the coal car to get through. He told me to jump out of the way of the mule and car as fast as I could. The mine was cut on a slope, and when the mule pullin' the coal car was trottin' he couldn't slow down. Miklos didn't jump back fast enough and the mule ran right over him, knockin' him to the ground and runnin' over him with the loaded coal car. There was nothin' anyone could do. We could hear Miklos screamin' back in the section of the mine where me and Pa was workin' that day. He didn't scream for long. He was dead by the time they carried him out of the mine.

Hard to believe that I been workin' in this mine goin' on thirteen years. Pa began havin' trouble breathin' last year, so I took over his job of settin' the charges and blastin' the coal. He taught me how to drill the holes deep enough to set the stick of dynamite, but not so deep that it would cause a whole wall of the mine to cave in. All of the men workin' the Central mine say that my pa was one of the best at blastin', and they said it was a real shame that he got miners' asthma and had to quit workin'.

I was actually happy for my pa. He would now have time to work the small farm we'd moved to back in 1891. Pa often told me the story of how he got the land in Frye Hollow, along with the farmhouse, from a distant cousin. The six-room farmhouse was much bigger than the little four-room shack he and Mum lived in when they were first married.

There was a bedroom for Pa and Mum, one for my three sisters, and another for me and my two brothers. The kitchen was real big and there was a livin' room, too. There was a front porch with a big swing to the right of the double front door, and the enclosed back porch was much like the one was at the little house. The outhouse had two stalls, so we didn't have to wait long if someone else had to use it.

Pa had asked a local farmer to plow a large area for Mum to put in a garden, and then me and Pa built a small chicken coop so we'd have fresh eggs. After we'd been livin' at the farmhouse for two years, the old man who had owned it died and no one laid claim to the property. Pa made the trip to the Westmoreland County Courthouse and filed for a deed for the house and property. Since no one contested the deed, it became our property after one year.

"James, this will be your place one day. Never forget how fortunate we were to get this little piece of land," Pa told me on the day we got the deed in the mail.

My day dreamin' ended when I got to the mine and I saw there were men gathered 'round the supply house. The mine superintendent, Mr. Bortz, was wavin' his hands, tryin' to get everyone's attention.

"Quiet down! Quiet! I have important news!" Mr. Bortz shouted.

Finally everyone stopped talkin' and all eyes turned to the superintendent, who was now standin' on a large keg.

"There was a mining accident yesterday at the Harwick mine in Cheswick. That mine is about sixteen miles north of Pittsburgh. The telegraph says it was a buildup of methane gas. At 8:15 a.m., when the workers blasted, the coal dust suspended in the air and traveled throughout every section of the mine. The force was so powerful that it wrecked the exterior of the shaft. Of the 179 miners underground at the time, there was only a single survivor, and he was severely burned. He was sixteen-year-old Adolph Gunia. He is not expected to live. Several more men died trying to rescue the trapped miners. I'm telling you all this to give warning of how dangerous the methane gas is. So be careful down there. The Hungarian community in Homestead, Pennsylvania was greatly impacted by this explosion. They lost fifty-eight men." Mr. Bortz wiped his eyes, and then continued: "I happen to know some of the men who died yesterday, and I want to have a moment of silence now to honor all those miners." Mr. Bortz bowed his head, as did every man standing there. "Go to work now, and may God be with you all," Mr. Bortz said as he jumped down from the keg.

I walked to the mine entrance, lit my carbide lantern, and climbed into the mantrip, which was pulled by a mule. The mantrip carried men and supplies into and out of the mine.

It wasn't as high as the coal cars, and it had benches for the men to sit on. When I first began workin' in the mine, me and Pa had to walk a mile or more into our section of the mine. Over the years, as more and more coal was being dug, the miners had to go deeper into the earth. Ridin' the mantrip gave the miners a reprieve from walkin' miles before beginnin' their shift. After a long day of diggin' coal, the mantrip was a time to let the body rest before startin' the long walk home from work.

Everyone was extremely quiet goin' into the mine. I guess each man had his mind on those who had died doin' the same job we do every day. I was sittin' next to an old Italian man who spoke broken English. When we got to the end of the rails that the mantrip traveled on, he climbed over the side, and then turned to look at me.

"God be with you!" he said.

"And with you, my friend," I replied.

I was surprised at how plainly he spoke these words. Although I could not understand him in general conversation, this phase was plain as could be.

The day passed slowly. I couldn't wait to get home and tell Pa about the Harwick disaster. I never told Mum about things that happen in the mine. Pa told me long ago to keep quiet about the dangers, for it would only make Mum worry more than she already does. However, I knew that Pa would hear all about this from some of the miners he talks with, and I wanted to be the first to tell him.

January in Western Pennsylvania is cold and snowy. This year there was an abundance of snow, which made walkin' through the fields a slow and exhausting process. Sarah was just comin' down the lane to our farm as I was steppin' out of the knee-deep snow and onto our lane. She's teachin' school in Hunker, a small community about two miles from home. I was surprised that she was so late comin' home.

"Ya be late this evenin', Sarah," I called out to her.

Sarah didn't answer me until she was a bit closer, so she wouldn't have to raise her voice.

"I had an interesting visitor come to the school when the children were just leaving. He came on the train from Latrobe. Said his name was Jamison, and he wanted information on some of the miners in our area," Sarah replied.

"What kind of information, and why ask a school teacher? Why didn't he just come to the mine and ask his questions?" I said.

"Well, he talked about the coal that is mined in our district and how it's ideal for gasification and conversion into coal gas. He said the Westmoreland Coal Company is looking into buying the controlling interest in Penn Gas Coal, a company that was established in 1861 to gasify coal. His family has been in the coal business for many years, and he is now interested in growing his business. He came to the school to talk with me and to see if this would be a suitable place for his workers to settle down. He wants to be able to tell them about all of the schools in this area. He said his grandfather is Robert Jamison. Do you know of him, James?" Sarah asked.

"No, I've never heard that name before, but I'll ask around. Maybe the superintendent has heard of him. Was he a nice fellow?" I asked.

"He seemed nice enough. He was dressed impeccably and spoke quite eloquently. I figured he was educated in a big city somewhere."

"Did he say if he'd be visitin' any of the mines?" I asked.

"No, he seemed more interested in the living conditions, the new hospital being built in Mount Pleasant, and the local schools. I guess that's why he wanted to speak with a school teacher instead of the mine owners," Sarah replied.

"Well, let me know if he comes back. If his grandfather owns a coal company, why is he travelin' by train? You'd think that he'd have his own coach and driver. Maybe his family isn't all that successful," I said.

"I don't know, but I bet Pa would know the name if they've been around since 1892. At least that's when Robert Jamison founded the Jamison Coal Company. Should I ask Pa about it?" Sarah asked.

"Yes, ask him about Jamison, and also ask him if he's heard anything about the mine strikes. Sometimes he talks with his old friends at the company store, although he doesn't walk there very often anymore. I'm sure glad Pa decided to move out here to Frye Hollow. I think the fresh air does him good," I replied.

"I'm glad, too, even though it's a bit longer for you to walk to work. I love country living. It's so much better than living in the patch," Sarah said.

As we got to the back porch, Benjamin and Jacob were washin' up. They're both workin' at the coke ovens, and they get just as dirty as I do in the mine. I sure am glad that Pa closed in the porch and hung a kerosene lantern on the wall, which provides both light and a bit of warmth for us as we clean ourselves each evening.

I could hear Delilah and Elizabeth talkin' in the kitchen. We don't often all get home for dinner at the same time, so the dinner table would be full of talkin' tonight. I'm sure Mum will be happy to have us all there together. She still worries over all of us like we're her little chicks and she's a mother hen.

Even Pa has been showin' signs of worry on his face, and he's lookin' older than his forty-four years. The miner's asthma is now bein' called "black lung" by Dr. Noon, and there isn't much he can do for Pa other than give him codeine cough syrup to sip when the coughing gets bad. Mum rubs Vicks on his neck and chest and he sleeps propped up with pillows.

Workin' in the mine since he was a young boy sure has taken its toll on my pa.

I wonder if I'll end up with black lung. I'm now a blaster just like Pa was. I breathe in the coal dust every day for twelve hours. When I look around the coal patch town of Central, I see many men with lung problems and arthritis.

I joined my brothers at the washtub, wishin' I'd gotten home first. I could wait for Mum to heat another pan of water on the coal stove, or I could wash with cold water, but my stomach made the decision for me. I was too hungry to wait any longer. The smell of fried chicken was makin' my mouth water. Guess the roosters were no longer needed in the hen house. Mum liked to cook them up before they got too old.

"Evenin', James. How was your day?" Pa asked as I walked into the kitchen, shirtless.

"I'll tell ya all 'bout it soon as I git a clean shirt on. Sarah had an interestin' day, too," I replied as I went to my bedroom for a clean shirt.

Mum likes for us to keep our work shirts on a nail above the washtub on the porch. She takes them down each mornin' for washin'. We don't have many shirts but Mum would never allow us to come to the dinner table dirty, even if it means that she has to do laundry every day.

Once we were all gathered around the table, Pa gave a short cough to signal everyone to quiet down. This was his way of sayin' it was time to pray.

"God, thank Ya for this food and for the hands that made it. Thank Ya for bringin' all the children home from work and school. Thank Ya for our family. In Jesus's name we pray. Amen."

I noticed that Pa's prayer this evening was short and to the point. Either he was anxious to hear about our days or smellin' that chicken cookin' made him as hungry as I'm sure the rest of us was.

"Sarah, you go first, and tell us 'bout your day," Pa said.

Sarah told Pa what she'd told me on our walk down the lane. All of the children listened without interruptin', which was unusual because they were always chatterin' 'bout something or other.

"I did hear of a man named Jamison. He was tryin' to start up his own mine back in '91. I heard his boys were workin' with 'im, but I don't know much else 'bout 'im," Pa replied.

"What do ya think he's up to, Pa?" I asked.

"Don't know, but it's none of our concern. A man has a right to ask questions, and maybe he's thinkin' on bringin' his family here to live. Sarah, did Mr. Jamison say he was comin' here to live?" Pa asked as he turned to look at Sarah.

"He didn't actually say that, but he talked about his workers coming to our area. He has something to do with using the gas created from coal, and he said the coal in our area is good for making gas. Do you know what coal gas is used for, Pa?" Sarah asked.

"I don't know much 'bout it. Might be that it burns cleaner than coal. Don't see no reason to be worried 'bout it. There's plenty of coal beneath us to mine. James, what did you want to tell us 'bout?" Pa asked.

"There was an accident at the Harwick mine in Cheswick yesterday. Mr. Bortz said it was an explosion caused by methane gas. He heard 179 men and boys were killed," I said.

"Oh, no. That's terrible news! Do ya have methane gas in the mine ya work in, James? " Mum cried.

"There's methane gas in all coal mines, Mum. We do our best to be safe, and we ventilate the mine as best we can. Don't be worryin' yourself 'bout this. Mr. Bortz says we're doin' a good job, and just hearin' 'bout this disaster gives us all cause to be extra careful," I replied.

"It's gettin' late, boys. Maybe we should all turn in for the night. Let's all remember to say a prayer for those who didn't make it out," Pa said as he pushed his chair back from the table.

As I stood up from my seat, my little sister Elizabeth got up and wrapped her arms 'round my belly.

"Ya won't blow up, will ya, James?" Elizabeth cried.

"Don't ya be afraid for me, Elizabeth. Every day before I go into the mine I ask God to keep me safe. Now ya just sleep well tonight, and dream happy dreams," I whispered in her ear.

As I climbed into my bed, I realized that I should have waited to tell Pa this news that I heard today. I figured Mum was the one to worry 'bout me, I didn't think Elizabeth would also be upset. I was surprised by her actions because she doesn't often hug me. It made me realize that my little sister is growin' up, too. From now on, I'll be more careful of my dinnertime conversations.

Benjamin and Jacob came in to bed shortly after me. I didn't want to continue the conversation from dinner, so I pretended to be asleep, but I did silently pray for a long time after I saw Pa put out all of the lamps.

When the house was all quiet, I thought I heard cryin' comin' from my parents' bedroom. I guess my mum feels as bad as I do about those who died in the Harwick coal mines, and I know that she fears for my safety.

CHAPTER THIRTEEN

WILLIAM MILLWARD

December 19, 1907 – Another Deadly Disaster

James came home from work this evenin' all excited. When he burst through the back door without even washin' up, I knew he must have somethin' important to tell us.

"Pa, there's been another deadly disaster this mornin' at the Darr Mine in Van Meter," James said between gasps to catch his breath.

"Where's Van Meter?" Anna asked.

"It's in Rostraver Township, which is also in Westmoreland County. It's only 'bout twelve miles from us," James replied. "There was a bad explosion, Pa. The mine superintendent spoke to someone at the Darr mine, and he said that, as near as they can figure, over 239 men and boys were killed. He said a lot more would have been killed, but today was a holy day, called the Feast of Saint Nickolas, so about two hundred men called off from work to go to the Greek Orthodox church. The bad thing is that some of the other men took their boys to work with them, to keep production up. Rumor has it that some of their wives also went to work with them today," James exclaimed.

"How did ya find out 'bout the accident if it just happened this mornin'? Anna asked.

"News spreads faster now than ever before thanks to the telephone, Mum. Up until 1899 most businesses had only a telegraph system, but now the American Telephone and Telegraph Company, AT&T, is installing telephones in all major businesses. I heard that someday everyone will have a telephone in their home," James replied.

"I don't see that happenin' anytime soon. It must cost a lot of money, and miners' don't have money," I said.

James put a lot of stock in the industrial revolution that's goin' on. I know he reads the newspaper any time he can get his hands on one, and he's adamant about the changes goin' on with the minin' companies. One of the problems that worries him most is the children that are bein' killed in the mines. Could be my fault that he worries so 'bout that, 'cause I took him to work with me when he was just nine years old. He never complained, and he worked hard for such a little lad. Yet every time there's a mine cave-in or explosion, James gets this faraway look in his eyes. So many times I've heard him say: "Another childhood lost, Pa."

"James, why don't ya go wash up, and I'll get your supper on the table," Anna said.

"I am gettin' hungry, Mum. I didn't have much of an appetite at lunchtime, just thinkin' 'bout all those men and boys at the Darr mine. I'll be right back," James replied as he rushed to the back porch.

"William, is the Central mine safe?" Anna asked once James was out of the kitchen.

"Safe as any of the other mines, I suppose. I've stressed to James how important it is to be very careful when he's in the mine, but accidents often happen without warnin'. Methane gas is one of the major reasons for explosions but there's also human error, too. The boy is twenty-five years old now, he knows his job and the dangers of it. We just have to pray every day that our son and all of the men and boys who work in the mine will have guardian angels with them," I replied.

I heard the voices of our other two sons, Benjamin and Jacob, comin' from the back porch. They usually get home earlier from the coke ovens than James does from the mine, but today they must have stopped at LaLa's Tavern to talk with some of the men from the mine.

Although Anna and I do not approve of the boys goin' to the tavern, they're old enough now to do as they please. As long as they just have a pint or two, and don't get all drunkard up, I know they're just lettin' off steam after a hard day's work. No doubt they'd already heard about the Darr mine explosion. Whenever there was a minin' accident anywhere it was cause for the miners to get together to discuss the matter.

Benjamin is twenty-four and Jacob is twenty-one years old now, makin' all of our sons men, but ya never stop worryin' 'bout 'em. The coke ovens have their share of accidents, too, but they aren't nearly as dangerous as bein' in the mines. Anna and I still pray for all of our children every mornin' when they go to work, and every night when we go to bed we thank God for bringin' 'em home to us. As we waited for the boys to get cleaned up and come to the supper table, I couldn't help but think of those poor women who wouldn't have their men folk come home this night. It was surely a sad day for a lot of people.

"Evenin', Mum! Evenin', Pa!" Benjamin and Jacob said as they came through the back door and took their seats at the table. James came in right behind them.

Anna put a large plate of fried pork chops in the middle of the table, along with a plate of fried potatoes and a bowl of homemade apple sauce. Sarah, Delilah, and Elizabeth had eaten their dinner much earlier. All three of our girls had gone to a neighbor's house to work on a quilt, so it would be a good time to discuss what had happened today with the boys.

Once everyone was seated around the table, Anna reached for my hand to signal that she was ready to say the blessin'.

"Dear God, Bless this food we are about to eat. Thank you for bringin' our boys safely home from work this day. We pray for all the souls lost in the Darr mine today, and we pray for their families, friends, and neighbors. In Jesus's name we pray. Amen."

"Amen!"

"James, tell us more of what you heard about the Darr Mine explosion," I asked.

"I heard that the whole Youghiogheny Valley shook when the blast occurred. The men were 'bout a mile-and-a-half down in the mine and couldn't get out 'cause the fire blew through all of the shafts. Some men from other mines went to help with the rescue and they said the stench of burnt mules and human bodies was terrible. No way to git any of 'em out until the fire burnt itself out. Then the rescuers were findin' just body parts and pieces of clothes. Some of the women were lookin' at anything the rescuers were bringin' out and sayin' if it was a hand, or a foot, or even a piece of long johns that looked like it might belong to their husbands or sons, they wanted to see it," James replied.

"Oh, how awful! I can't imagine having to look at severed body parts to try and find one of you," Mum cried.

"Maybe we'd better talk 'bout this later, boys. Your mum is gettin' upset by all the gruesome details," I replied

"No, please go on, James. I want to know what's happening at the mines. After all, I have a stake in this, since my sons work at the mine and the coke ovens," Mum said.

"Well, Mum, I don't want to upset ya more. I also heard that there isn't enough room in any one cemetery to bury all of the dead, so the bodies are bein' taken to several areas. Some went to Connellsville, Scottdale, and Smithton. There were seventy-one unidentified bodies and body parts that were put in a mass grave at the Olive Branch Cemetery. Many of the people didn't have enough money to bury their dead, and the mine owners wouldn't pay for individual cemetery plots. I'm sure there will be more mass graves in the next few days," James said.

"It's a damn shame how those owners treat the men!" Benjamin shouted.

"Now, Ben, don't be swearin' and gettin' excited," I said.

"Sorry, Mum! Didn't mean no disrespect, but it isn't right how the men with the money have no regard for the workers. I've heard it said that a mine owner said he could replace any man 'cause there's always more immigrants wantin' to come to America to work. They feel that a mule or pony is more valuable than a man. If they can't git all of the bodies out of that section of the mine they'll just blast it shut and then dig another shaft along the coal seam in another area," Ben replied.

"Is that true, William?" Anna asked.

"Yes, I'm afraid it is. Many of the mine owners are cavalier and ruthless. They look only to the profit they make, not how many have to die to give them that profit. An animal costs them money; the men come freely to work and slave in the mines," I said.

"Do you remember, Mum, when the miners formed the United Mine Workers in 1890 to gain power and win their demands for safety and more pay? The UMWA fought for the miners and won a nationwide bituminous strike and gained the eight-hour day and operators' recognition of the union as the collective bargaining agent for many miners in Western Pennsylvania, Ohio, Indiana, and Illinois. None of that matters here in southwestern Pennsylvania 'cause our mine is so small that if we don't do what the bosses want, they'll just fire us and git a new group of immigrants off the next boat comin' into Ellis Island. We're considered disposable to those greedy, rich bastards," James exclaimed.

"James! I've asked you boys to watch ya mouth. I won't allow cursin' in front of ya mum!" I shouted.

I rarely raise my voice to my children, so they all sat up straighter and looked at me with wide eyes and mouths agape. Anna also looked a bit shocked by my outburst, but I meant business. I've heard enough of foul-mouth talkin' at the mine and I will not have it in my home.

"Sorry, Mum," James and Benjamin said in unison.

"Maybe we should change the subject. Talkin' 'bout all the death and sorrow is makin' me sad. Benjamin, how was your day?" Anna asked.

"My day was the same as it always is. I drive the engine, called a 'dinkie,' that pulls the larry car across the top of the coke ovens. The larry drops a load of coal into the coke oven through a hole at the top," Benjamin replied.

"Yeah, and then I reach in through the door in the front of the oven with a rake and scrape the coal level so that it burns evenly. The oven that I charge is between two hot ovens, so that the newly-charged oven can light itself by spontaneous combustion," Jacob said.

"How do ya know when the coke is ready to take out of the oven?" Mum asked.

"When the coal that is still wet from cleanin' is first charged into the oven, it begins to steam. Next, I put the damper on at the top and seal the oven door almost all the way up with bricks and mud. Then I watch the escaping smoke as it turns blue, then a thick yellow. 'Bout an hour later, the coal will catch fire, and then it will explode and you can see the fire spread all over the inside of the oven. When it settles down, I take a tool called a hook and pull the damper back. The art of making good coke is in controlling the damper and the height of the oven door, to regulate the burning of the coal inside the oven. Usually in seventy-two hours all of the impurities are baked out of the coal and good coke remains. To unload, or 'pull' the ovens, the brick door is taken down with the hook and the coke is sprayed with water to stop the baking process. Then the coke is lifted out with a big fork, loaded into wheelbarrows, and dumped into the flatcars," Jacob explained.

I could see that all three of my sons were proud of the work that they do at the Central Coal and Coke Company. Just listenin' to 'em tell their mum what they do each day gives me a sense of pride, too. I was glad that Jacob didn't go into more detail of how hot the coke oven gets or how dangerous it can be. Better to let Anna think that her boys that work the coke ovens are a bit safer than the son who works inside the mine. No need to tell her of how the steam that bellows out of the ovens when the coal's dampened could burn the skin right off of a man's face, or how breathin' in the putrid-smellin' coke could cause miner's asthma just as sure as workin' inside the mine could.

Every aspect of workin' in the coal industry is dangerous and, oftentimes, deadly. I knew this when I worked years ago back in Wales, and even though we were promised a better life here in America, nothin' has really changed.

"I know my boys work so hard, and I'm proud of ya all. Now, ya best all git to bed. Mornin' comes much too fast in the winter months. Seems like ya never git to see daylight," Anna replied.

Just then I heard laughin' and feet stompin' off the snow from boots on the back porch as our three girls came home from their quiltin' bee. James was the first to jump into action, and went out onto the porch to greet his sisters. Benjamin and Jacob joined him, with mischievous grins on their handsome faces. The snow that was on the floor was quickly scooped up in the boys' large hands and then they put the snow on the girls' necks, just under the scarves they were trying to take off.

It was good to hear our children teasin' each other. They all have to work so hard just to help us make a livin', and this good-natured banterin' will be a memory that they'll keep close to their precious hearts for the rest of their lives. *I silently thanked God for these children and for another day that has brought them all safely home.*

CHAPTER FOURTEEN

ANNA MILLWARD

June 1, 1908 – Better Days Ahead

"I'm home, Mum!" Sarah called out as she came through the front door.

"I'm in the kitchen, Sarah. Come and tell me 'bout your day," I replied.

It's hard to think of my three daughters as women, but that's exactly what they've become. I enjoy hearin' 'bout the things that make them happy. Sarah's been courtin' a man from New Stanton named Jeremiah Laufenberg and I've never seen her in better spirits.

Our Sunday afternoons have become quiet lately. William and I don't always go to church, but the girls enjoy the morning services and the afternoon socials held once a month. Sarah came home from the social today all excited.

"Jeremiah's pa is courtin' a lady from Central and you'll never guess who it is!" Sarah said excitedly.

"Now, Sarah, ya know I don't like to gossip 'bout people," I said.

"Mum, I'm not gossipin'. In fact, Jeremiah told me weeks ago 'bout his pa seein' someone, and I haven't told a soul. Not even you! So now that Mr. Laufenberg has told Jeremiah that he and his lady friend are goin' to announce their weddin' soon I thought it would be a good time to tell you. Today Mr. Laufenberg brought Gretchen Klink to the church social for the first time. Oh, Mum, I'm so happy for them. They seem so in love," Sarah replied.

I had to laugh to myself. Sarah thought this was her and Jeremiah's little secret, when in fact I'd known all along about Mr. Laufenberg and the woman he'd fallen in love with. I, too, can keep secrets, and that's exactly what I've been doin' for several months now.

Jeremiah's mother died a few years ago. Karl Laufenberg was very lonely without his wife. Karl and Jeremiah run the small grocery store and meat market, but it seems so empty without a woman's touch.

"Well, Sarah, I've known 'bout Gretchen's beau for some time. I didn't want to tell anyone until she and Karl were ready to let everyone else know 'bout their plans," I whispered.

"Oh, Mum, I thought I was gonna surprise ya," Sarah said, laughingly.

"Ya know, Sarah, ya should know me well enough by now to see that I don't talk 'bout people. Gretchen's always been a very private person, and I respect her feelings," I replied.

Just then Delilah and Elizabeth came into the kitchen. They both stopped short at hearing my last words to Sarah.

"What's wrong with Miss Klink?" they both asked at once.

"If you'd come to the church social with us today instead of goin' berry pickin' you'd know what is goin' on with Miss Klink," Sarah replied.

"See! That's how fast gossip gets started. Someone says somethin', another couple people hear part of the conversation, and it carries on from there," I laughed.

"We're not gossipin', Mum, and there's nothin' wrong with Miss Klink. In fact, she's doin' wonderful. She's gonna marry Mr. Laufenberg," Sarah told her sisters.

The girls formed a group hug, squealin' and dancin' 'round the kitchen. I had to laugh at seein' them goin' in circles like they did as small children playin' Ring Around the Rosie. It warms my heart to know that my daughters, who are now women, can still enjoy the closeness of their sisterhood.

Delilah works at the company store, keepin' the books, and Elizabeth seems content to stay at home with me, cookin' and cleanin'. She still enjoys gatherin' the eggs from the hen house, just like she did as a little girl. Elizabeth also has a green thumb; everything she touches in the garden seems to grow bigger and better than ever. God has truly blessed us with six wonderful children. I only wish that life could be a bit easier for them, especially for our boys.

"If Miss Klink marries Mr. Laufenberg, will she no longer be the midwife here in Central and Rocktown?" Delilah asked.

"Jeremiah said that she will most likely move to New Stanton. They need her help with the store and meat market. Now that the railroad has established daily passenger and freight service, and there's a streetcar which runs between Uniontown and Greensburg, too. New Stanton now encompasses two villages, Old Stanton and Paintersville. Business and travel are growin' by leaps and bounds. They even have a post office that has one of the first two Rural Free Delivery systems in the United States," Delilah explained.

"Well you really seem to know a lot about New Stanton, Delilah," Elizabeth said.

"Oh, I just listen to Jeremiah tellin' me all 'bout the history of his family comin' to America from Germany. He's so interestin', and he just thrives on American history. Mum, did you know that the flour mill here was built in 1852 by Colonel Isaac Painter, one of the five men who also developed the southwest branch of the Pennsylvania Railroad?" Delilah replied.

"The only thing I know about New Stanton is that the United Church of Christ was just finished, in 1906, on land donated by James and Catharine Stanton. Mrs. Stanton saved egg money to buy the church a bell. That's what Miss Hodgekiss told us in school one day," Elizabeth said.

"Yes, I guess New Stanton is becoming a very busy little town. I'm sure Gretchen and Karl will make a good living together there," I replied

"Mum, Jeremiah and I have been talkin' about his father's store. If we should get married someday, how would ya feel if I moved to New Stanton?" Sarah asked.

Delilah and Elizabeth began huggin' Sarah once more, but this time they were cryin' instead of laughin'. I wasn't at all surprised by Sarah's statement. In fact, I'd wondered what had taken her so long to begin talkin' 'bout marriage. Most women are long-married by the time they are twenty-four years old.

"I'd be mighty proud of ya both. I'm sure that the store and meat market could provide for both of the Laufenberg men and their wives," I said

With all of the laughin' and cryin' goin' on with the girls, none of us heard William come into the kitchen. I looked up to see him wipin' his eyes on his shirt sleeve. Sarah looked from me to her father. Suddenly she, too, was cryin' as she ran to William and wrapped her arms around him.

"Seems like my little girl is all grown up!" William said.

"I'll always be your little girl, Pa," Sarah whispered in William's ear.

"It's time we start gettin' supper ready, girls," I said.

Everyone has a job to do to prepare for the evenin' meals. Elizabeth sets the table while Delilah goes to the root cellar to fetch some canned apple sauce. Even though our supply is runnin' low, we need to use up all of the old stock to make room for this year's crop. We'd been blessed when we moved to Frye Hollow to have good, fertile land and a creek to water the garden in summer months when it's hot and dry.

The cinders from the coke ovens blew across the valleys, droppin' smoke and ash onto the trees and plants below. The farmers say this is the best fertilizer and it also kept the bugs off of the plants. Even the wild berry bushes are abundant this year.

I was lookin' forward to see just how many berries the boys would bring home. I expected them to be here any minute. Delilah and Elizabeth had come home earlier and neither of them had been carryin' the pail they used for berry pickin'. I just hoped that the boys hadn't eaten all of the berries on the walk home.

The roast beef I'd put in the oven a few hours ago was so tender that it was fallin' apart. I'd put fresh carrots and potatoes around it just before the girls got home and caused all of the commotion. The kitchen smelled wonderful, and I couldn't wait to have all of my children around the table to enjoy my preparations.

Just like clockwork, the boys arrived as I was placin' the food on a large meat platter. Sunday evening is our family time. Durin' the week, when everyone is workin', our meals are eaten in shifts, as the family gets home, but Sunday is the Lord's Day. We all make sure that our daily plans don't interfere with this special time. William and I insist on this. When we came to America we gave up so much—many of our family members were either deceased or still in Wales—and we want our children to have a good sense of family and commitment. This is and will always be a priority, as long as our children reside under our roof. We do realize that once they get married and have families of their own, this may change.

"William, will ya say the blessin', please!" I asked.

"Dear Lord, we thank Ya for this food, and for the hands that have prepared it. We thank Ya for the bounty of the earth, for our family and friends, and for good health. Be with our children as they go to work this comin' week. Bless our friend, Gretchen Klink, and her soon-to-be husband, Karl. May they have a long and happy life. In Jesus's name we pray. Amen!"

"William, did you know 'bout Gretchen and Karl, too?" I asked.

"Well, I did hear some of your conversation with the girls, but a man would have to be blind to not notice how Karl looks at Gretchen. I may not go to church every Sunday, but the times I have gone, I've seen 'the look' in his eye. Sure didn't surprise me none to hear 'bout weddin' plans," William replied.

"Oh, and you were worried 'bout me startin' gossip, Mum," Sarah said.

"Well, I still think you all should keep this quiet until Gretchen and Karl want to announce their plans to the communities," I said.

"What's goin' on, Mum?" James asked.

"Here we go again!" I laughed.

Sarah went on to explain to her brothers what we'd all been talkin' about this afternoon, and she also told them how I'd reprimanded them for gossipin'. Yet no one seemed at all surprised to hear the news of Gretchen and Karl. It seems that the whole town of Central was already talkin' 'bout their midwife. James had heard 'bout it at the mine. Benjamin and Jacob heard 'bout it at the coke ovens, and William finally admitted to me that he'd heard 'bout it at the feed mill in New Stanton. Was I the only one to keep a secret around here?

"Awe, Mum. Ya did your best to keep Gretchen's secret. Ya be a good friend, but others tend to talk 'bout what they see, and they've seen Karl and Gretchen in church and visitin' each other. They've just put two and two together and figured it out. I'm sure that Gretchen knows what a good and faithful friend ya be," James said.

"Yes, I guess you're right," I replied.

I walked outside to sit on the swing under the grape arbor. The girls would finish cleanin' up the supper dishes. I needed time to think. My friends were movin' on.

When Colleen O'Malley left our neighborhood, I missed her so much. The death of her son caused me to fear for my own children more. I love Colleen and her family dearly. It's hard to understand why she has never returned to see me and has never written to me. I guess the memories of Rocktown are just too painful for her.

Now Gretchen will be leavin' soon. She has helped to deliver every one of my babies, and we've been close friends for goin' on twenty-six years. Even though New Stanton isn't that far away, she will be very busy with her new life as a storekeeper's wife.

When William and I left Rocktown and moved to Frye Hollow we still were in close contact with our friends and neighbors of the "patch." William still saw the men at the coal mine, and I still saw some of my friends at the Mount Lebanon Methodist Church of Tarrs. I still go to the company store once or twice a month for supplies that I can't make or grow myself. Although James is still paid in script at the mine, we've been successful at sellin' our meats and vegetables for cash money.

Although we'll always be poor, we're rich in what matters most: our love of family.

God has blessed us, and I'm grateful for His love and mercy.

CHAPTER FIFTEEN

JAMES D. MILLWARD

January 2, 1912 – Recollections

My pa would have been fifty-two years old this year. I don't know why I was thinkin' on the past. The past can't be changed, and the future is up to God. We have no control over what will happen next in the coal mine or anywhere else, for that matter.

We're born into this world, we work, we struggle to survive, and then we die.

Pa died much too young. Right after Christmas he got influenza which, combined with the miner's asthma, made it extremely hard for him to breathe. Mum did all she could for him. She'd rub his chest with Vicks salve, give him the tonic ol' Doc Noon prescribed. She even made a small tent, from a piece of an ol' canvas tarp—she'd boil water and Pa would sit at the table, holdin' that canvas tent over his head and breathin' in the hot steam, tryin' to loosen up the congestion in his chest. Nothin' worked, and his last night in bed with Mum he coughed so hard that his heart just gave out. Mum is a widow at forty-six years old.

"Hey, Jim! Wait up and I'll walk with ya!" Bob Meyers shouted.

Bob lives along the road between the Central mine and Frye Hollow. He came to the area a few years ago with his wife Jane. They're due to have their first baby soon.

"Mornin', Bob. How's your wife doin'?" I asked.

"She's gettin' big as a barrel. We should have us a baby any day now. How many of your brothers are still livin' on the farm?" Bob asked.

"All of the children except me and Elizabeth have married and moved on. We still live in the farmhouse in Frye Hollow, but I've been thinkin' on movin' closer to the mine. There are some old company houses close to the coke ovens that have been abandoned, and Mr. Frick said that he'd like them torn down. I plan on goin' to the mine office this mornin' to see if I can have the wood as payment for doin' the demolition," I replied.

"What ya plannin' to do with that old used wood?" Bob asked.

"There's a piece of land next to the Snydertown Tavern that's for sale. It would be a good place to build a house, and it's less than a mile to the Tarrs church. I'm sure my mum would like to be able to walk to church every Sunday. Even in winter she could walk on the road, unlike bein' at Frye Hollow where she has to walk across a field of drifted snow for a mile before she can get to a main road. Since Pa is buried up at the Tarrs cemetery, I know Mum would also like to visit his grave," I explained.

"Do ya plan on sellin' the farm if ya move?" Bob asked

"I haven't told Mum my plans yet. It's better to talk with Mr. Frick first and see if I can afford the land. I'll need to discuss this with Elizabeth as well. Of course my other brothers and sisters will also have to be consulted 'bout our move, but if none of them want the farm, then I think we may consider sellin' it," I said.

"I'd appreciate it if you'd let me know if ya want to sell the place. Jane and I will be needin' a bigger place once the baby is born," Bob replied.

"I'll let ya know as soon as I can," I said.

We walked the rest of the way to work in silence. I had been in a melancholy mood before Bob showed up, and that hadn't changed since our short conversation. I just couldn't stop thinkin' 'bout the past.

I can't remember bein' a child. It seems like I've been workin' hard all my life. The cold wind feels like it's blowin' right through me. My soul even feels cold today. I don't much like feelin' this way, but don't know how to stop these thoughts from creepin' into my head. I've been workin' in the mine for twenty-one years. Some of my closest friends have died or left the coal patch town of Central.

Maybe my thoughts are due to the nightmares I still have from time to time 'bout Patrick O'Malley. I never got a chance to talk with Patrick before he died. We were mad at each other when he ran away, and he didn't say goodbye. I heard Mum tellin' my pa that Patrick had suffered much, havin' one leg cut off and the other foot crushed by the wheels of a train. I often think of him when I hear the train whistle at the Tarrs railroad crossin'.

There have been many children who have died workin' in the coal mines. Some of them I knew, and some I just heard the horrendous stories of how they met their demise.

"Hey, Jim, I just read a newspaper article 'bout a man named Lewis Hine, an investigative photographer. He went to many mines and factories takin' photographs of the nation's children at work. Child labor is becomin' an important issue to a group of Americans that call themselves Progressives. They are tryin' to stop the use of children in the workforce, especially in dangerous industries such as coal mining. Have ya heard anything 'bout 'em?" Bob asked.

"No, can't say that I have. I went to work in the mine when I was nine years old. My pa wouldn't have liked someone tellin' him I couldn't work. We needed the money," I said.

"Well, this Mr. Hine went to Eastern Pennsylvania where the coal is called anthracite. It burns longer and hotter than the bituminous coal here in Western Pennsylvania. There he photographed boys as young as six years old workin' as breaker boys. Coal moves from the top of the breaker down chutes. The boys sit over the chutes on planks of wood, one boy lower than the next. There was a picture of those little guys in the paper. Whatever slate and other rocks the boys on the upper levels miss, the ones below them are to catch. Slate looks similar to coal, so the boys have to bend over to closely inspect the movin' rocks. They got gloves to protect their hands, but in some breakers the bosses won't let the boys wear them—the gloves make it harder to pick out smaller rocks. Even with the gloves, jagged edges sometimes pierce the cloth and cut the little boys' hands. Mr. Hine explained all this in the newspaper so people would feel sorry for the young'uns," Bob replied.

"Did this Hine fella really take photographs, or did he just sketch the pictures for the paper?" I asked.

"Sure did look like real photographs in that newspaper. Hine wrote that he saw the thick coal dust that filled the breaker. He said that it went so deep into the boys' lungs that they continued to cough up the black coal dust even after leavin' work. He even took a photograph of a group of boys comin' out of Ewen Breaker when they stopped for lunch. Showed how the boys are of many ages and sizes, dressed in almost the same way. They were all covered in coal dust. Hine said he wanted millions of Americans to see how the children of the coal patch towns have to work and suffer," Bob said.

"I wonder why this Mr. Hine didn't come to our coal mine. It isn't just the children in the East who are sufferin'.

We're all gonna have black lung from breathin' in the coal dust," I replied.

As we got nearer to the mine office, I turned to Bob and put out my hand. I wanted to speak to Mr. Frick alone, if he was in his office.

"God be with ya, Bob," I said.

"To you as well, Jim," Bob replied as he swiftly walked towards the mine shaft.

I don't hear many men say a miner's blessin' anymore. My pa would never even think of goin' into the mine without sayin' it. I can't change my ways now—I truly believe in askin' for God's blessin' for a safe day. I don't even know if Bob Meyers is a Christian or not, but no matter, I will ask God to watch out for us all.

I knocked on the office door before enterin' and then opened the latch. Mr. Frick was talkin' to a mine superintendent, and he waved at me to have a seat in a chair beside the pot-belly stove in the corner of the room.

"How can I help you, Jim?" Mr. Frick asked.

"Well, sir, I heard ya be wantin' some of the old houses torn down. I was wonderin' if you'd be willin' to let me have the old lumber in exchange for the demolition of two or three of the houses?" I asked.

"I think that's a reasonable deal. What are you planning on doing with all that used lumber?" Mr. Frick asked.

"Well, since my pa passed on, the farm is too big for Mum and my sister to keep up. I'd like to look into the land next to Snydertown Tavern. There's enough room there for two houses. I hope to marry someday, and I'd want a place of my own." I explained.

"Have you talked with the landowner on the price?" Mr. Frick asked.

"Not yet. I first wanted to see if you would let me have the used wood," I replied.

"Jim, you and your family have been hard-working, loyal employees. Let me approach the owner of the tavern and negotiate a fair price for the land. After all, buying and selling property is my business. Then we can talk about you paying me for the property by working extra hours," Mr. Frick explained.

"Mr. Frick, what percentage of profit would ya want to charge me?" I asked.

"You're a smart man, Jim. If I can get that piece of property for a good price, I'll only charge a minimal percent. Oh, let's say two percent. Does that sound like a good deal?" Mr. Frick asked.

"I'd like to talk with the owner first, and then I'll let ya know if I think it's a good deal," I said as I turned to leave the office. I didn't want to be late for my shift in the mine.

"I like you, Millward!" Mr. Frick laughed as I walked outside.

I hurried down into the mine to begin my day of blastin'. As I worked I couldn't stop thinkin' on all Bob and I had talked 'bout on our way to work. I'd have to see if I could borrow that newspaper Bob had. I'm surprised that anyone is interested in the welfare of all the children that have to work in dangerous jobs.

Bein' that I was one of those children makes the story more interestin' to me. However, I do question how these people called Progressives will make things any better for the coal miners. If the children can't work, how will the miners' families make enough money to live? Unless the mine owners change how they pay the miners, life will not get better in the patch. Bein' paid by script will still keep the miners slaves to the coal companies.

It would be nice for the youngest boys to have some sort of childhood. Seems like my days of goin' fishin', playin' ball, and just bein' a boy were taken from me when I was nine. Pa would never let Mum baby me, either. He said I had to be a man and do a man's work, and that I didn't need my mum wipin' my nose at every little bump or callus.

When my pa died, I held my mum in my arms while she cried. I know it seems mean to think it, but I enjoyed bein' hugged by my mum. I didn't feel that it was a sign of weakness. It was my way of givin' her support and love.

Maybe now I could give my mum a hug more often. Yep, Bob really got me to thinkin' on the children of the coal mines. I hope I can see those photographs of Mr. Hine. I don't doubt that I'll see a portrait of myself in those children's eyes.

CHAPTER SIXTEEN

PEARL WOLFORD

September 26, 1912 – The Barn Dance

I didn't plan on goin' to no "barn dance" but my sister kept after me 'bout it. She'd give me no peace 'til I agreed to walk her to the Funk farm, just a mile from our place in Frye Hollow.

"Now, Pearl, ya go to that dance and find a nice man to marry. Ya be twenty-four years old now, an old maid," Mum shouted at me when she heard me tellin' Daisy that I didn't want to go with her.

"Mum, I don't plan on meetin' any men. I'll walk with Daisy just to be sure she'll be safe in this stupid place, but I won't make friends. I don't know why we had to leave England to come here!" I shouted.

"Young lady, you mind your manners!" Mum shouted back.

That's the way it always is now that we've moved to America: Mum and me are always at odds with each other. I can't do anything to please her, and all she thinks about is gettin' her daughters married off. Bein' that I'm the oldest, I get the brunt of her temper in every instance. Daisy seems to do no wrong in Mum's eyes. Well, maybe I should just jump on the first man I see and get married. Then Mum will see just how much her precious little Daisy does. I've always been the daughter that does the most around the house. I can't picture Daisy milkin' the cow or hoein' the garden.

"Come on, Daisy! I'll go with ya!" I said.

"Pearl, aren't ya goin' to put on a nice dress and fix your hair?" Daisy cried.

"I said I'd go with ya, I didn't say I'd get all fancied up," I replied.

"Mum, tell Pearl to fix herself up!" Daisy yelled.

I stomped up the steps to my bedroom on the second floor of the farmhouse we'd just moved into last month. I knew it would do no good to argue with Mum on this. She'd just make my life miserable if I didn't go with Daisy, and Daisy would make me miserable if I didn't try to look the part of a woman searchin' for a husband.

I put on my best Sunday dress and combed my long, dark brown hair. I didn't have any new hair ribbons so I just let my hair fall over my shoulders. I didn't even look in the mirror above my dresser because I really didn't care how I looked. After all, who was there to impress but a bunch of old farm boys and some coal miners? They were used to lookin' at the rump of a mule, so no matter what I did with my hair, I'd still be presentable.

"That's better, Pearl. Ya look beautiful! Now go and have a good time," Mum said as I came down the stairs.

"Pearl, I've never been to a barn dance. Do ya know what they do there?" Daisy asked.

"Can't say that I know what they'll do. I guess dance in a barn," I replied.

"Oh, you're so funny, Pearl. I know they'll be dancin', but I wonder what else there will be to do," Daisy replied.

Daisy was so excited to be gettin' out of the house that she practically skipped the whole mile across the fields to the farm. I walked a bit slower, to be alone with my thoughts.

I really am not a very social person. I don't like church socials, or quiltin' bees, or wastin' time talkin' with women in the yard between the clotheslines. Mum always called me unsociable, but I just never thought of myself as havin' anything interesting to say.

When the barn came into sight, Daisy ran back and grabbed my hand.

"Hurry, Pearl. I don't want to walk into the barn all by myself. Please hurry!" Daisy said.

"Daisy, don't act too forward. Ya don't want everyone there to think you've never been to a dance before," I whispered.

"Well, I haven't been to a barn dance before. Oh, I hope there will be boys my age here. Do you think there'll be anyone my age?" Daisy asked.

I thought maybe she was getting a case of cold feet and would change her mind about goin' into the barn.

"I'm sure there will be at least one eighteen-year-old here," I replied.

Just as we stepped around to the front of the barn, two young men came runnin' past us and almost knocked me over. I was flabbergasted!

What hooligans, I thought to myself.

"Oh, I'm so sorry! I'm Mary Funk, and those are my twins, Tommy and Toby."

Mrs. Funk was a small woman with red hair and freckles across her nose. She'd come out of the barn just as we were tryin' to enter it.

"No harm done, Mrs. Funk. I'm Daisy Wolford, and this is my sister Pearl," Daisy said.

"I'm so glad you could come. Are your parents going to come to the dance as well?" Mrs. Funk asked.

"No, they are still quite busy gettin' the house in order. We've only been in America a month. In fact, Mum said to tell you that she's lookin' forward to meetin' ya soon, and to thank ya for havin' me and Daisy over tonight," I replied.

"I'm so glad you both came. Please come inside and get a cool glass of apple cider. The music will begin once everyone has eaten dinner. I hope you like fried chicken," Mrs. Funk said.

Daisy was already at the big, wooden barrel by the time I'd finished talkin' to Mrs. Funk. A tall, skinny boy with freckles was pourin' her a glass of cider and she was grinning like a Cheshire cat. So much for my advice on not pushin' herself on the men. 'Course Daisy didn't have to push herself on anyone, she's a real beauty. Pa always called her his "Little Princess" and she sure does live up to that title.

Daisy and the young man took their drinks and moved to the back of the barn where some benches were leaning against the wall. I watched as she looked up into the young man's eyes, and laughed. It was goin' to be a long evening tryin' to keep her in line. Mum would be furious if she saw how bold Daisy was bein' with this boy.

I was just reachin' for a glass when a large, calloused hand folded around my hand. Although the man smelled clean, his hands were the color of coal and sulfur—part black, part dark red. There was no mistakin' that he was a coal miner. He was so tall that I had to look up to see his face, which is uncommon for me because I'm a tall woman myself.

"May I pour you a drink, miss?" he asked.

"Thank you," I replied.

He got me the cool apple cider and I took a drink at once. Suddenly it got very warm in this drafty ol' barn. I wasn't sure of what to say to this big man, and I didn't want to appear too forward, so I just let him lead me to the benches on the opposite side of the barn from my sister.

"My name's Jim. I haven't seen you 'round here before. What's your name?" he asked.

"I'm Pearl Wolford. We just moved to Frye Hollow last month," I said.

"Did ya move into the ol' farm at the end of Trout Lane?" Jim asked.

"Yes, how did ya know?" I asked.

"That used to be our home. Until my pa died, that is. I built a house for my mum and sister which is closer to the Tarrs church. The farm was too far for Mum to walk in the winter," Jim replied.

"How nice of ya to be so carin' of your family. Do ya live with your mum?" I asked, and then I felt my face get hot with embarrassment. How could I be so bold?

"No, I put up a small shack beside Mum and Elizabeth's house. I've lived with my parents all my life until just this summer. I figured it was time to live alone. How 'bout you? Do ya live with your parents?" Jim said.

"Yes, we just moved here from England," I replied.

"Who does 'we' consist of? Do ya have a large family?" Jim asked.

"Not a large family—just my parents and me and my sister Daisy. She's over there on that bench with the red-haired young man," I said.

"That young man is Jared Funk. His parents own this farm, and they do have a very large family. Your sister has good taste in men," Jim laughed.

"Well, it didn't take her long to meet that one. We were no sooner in the door than he was pourin' her a drink of cider," I said.

"You'll find that in a coal minin' and farmin' community, men don't have time for long courtships. Ya never know what tomorrow will bring, so most live for today."

We sat for awhile in silence, just sippin' our cider and watchin' all of the other people wander in from outside. I tried to get a good look at Jim while he was observin' his friends and neighbors. I thought him to be very handsome upon close inspection. I wondered why he'd want to keep company with me.

I'm very plain, almost homely by most standards. I've got a big, round nose and bushy eyebrows. I guess my lips are presentable: full and naturally pink. Mum has always said that Daisy is the pretty one and I'm the practical daughter. Sittin' so close to this handsome Welsh man, I began to feel like a normal woman. Maybe there's hope for me to find a husband.

Mrs. Funk came to the door of the barn and began ringin' a big, brass bell. Once everyone stopped talkin' to see what the ringin' was all about, she announced that the food was ready and that there were tables and benches set up outside.

Jim stood up and smiled at me. He offered me his arm, givin' me the courtesy of walkin' beside him to where the food was set out. As we neared the picnic area I was amazed at how much food there was. Large platters of fried chicken sat in the middle of the long servin' table, along with bowls of potato salad, cucumber salad, and corn on the cob. There were Mason jars of garden relish and succotash.

It would be very hard to be ladylike and only eat a small portion of food with such a large spread of victuals before me. Everything smelled amazin' and I realized that I hadn't eaten anything since breakfast this mornin'.

Jim let me go before him in the line of hungry guests. My mouth was waterin' so much that I had to keep lickin' my lips. I took a small portion of everything that was on the table, and when I turned to see if Jim was close by me, I realized that he must be hungry, too. There were long tables made from boards laid across sawhorses, with handmade benches on both sides of the tables. We sat beside each other, and Jim moved close to me to make room for another coal miner and his girl.

I'd never seen a man eat so much! Jim must have taken two of everything there was to offer, and he wasted no time in gettin' his plate clean.

"What is your favorite food, Pearl?" Jim asked.

"I liked the fried chicken best, but it was all delicious. What was your favorite?" I asked.

"I don't have any one favorite, I just love all food. Potatoes seem to be the most plentiful year-round. I guess I like them most any way Mum could think of cookin' em," Jim replied.

Just as we were gettin' up from the table, a group of men went inside the barn and began tunin' up their instruments. One man had a guitar, another a banjo, and another was blowin' on a mouthorgan. We were walkin' towards the barn door when a young man with a fiddle pushed past us to join the band.

The sun was just beginnin' to set when the dancin' got in full swing. First, the band played a fast and snappy tune that sounded like Irish music, and then they began playin' a waltz.

"I don't know how to dance, but I'd sure like to try if ya don't mind?" Jim said.

"I've never danced before, but it doesn't look that hard to do. Most of the couples are just walkin' round the barn holdin' onto each other's shoulders. I'll try not to step on your toes," I whispered.

"Good! We'll learn to dance together," Jim replied.

It felt so good to be held in Jim's strong arms. I could feel the muscles of his shoulders through his thin cotton shirt. He was so tall that my head rested on his chest, just below his chin. When we were watchin' the young people dance, they stood arms'-length apart, but as soon as the music slowed, Jim pulled me closer and rested his chin upon the top of my head. I could hear his heart beatin' and I felt butterflies in my stomach. I don't know if he was feelin' the same way, but it sure was a wonderful evenin'.

The band announced that they'd play one more song, and then the barn dance would be over. The evenin' had gone by much too fast and I'd forgotten all about keepin' an eye on Daisy.

While we were dancin' our last dance, Jim pulled me closer and leaned down to whisper in my ear: "Can I see ya again, Pearl?" he asked.

"Yes, I'd like that. You know where I live, so when would ya like to come callin'"? I asked.

"I only have one day a week off work, so is next Sunday a good time to visit?" Jim asked.

"Yes! Would ya like to come for dinner?" I said.

"What time does your family have dinner?" Jim replied.

"We always eat as soon as we get home from church around one o'clock," I said.

When the music stopped Jim and I were still standin' in the middle of the barn, holdin' each other.

"Pearl Wolford! Are ya ready to go home?" Daisy said with a big grin on her face.

"Jim, this is my sister, Daisy. Daisy, this is Jim Millward," I said with an equally big grin on my face.

"Shall I walk you ladies home?" Jim asked.

"Ya can walk if ya want to, but Jared has offered us a ride in his buggy. I'm sure the horse can pull four people as easily as two, don't ya think, Mr. Millward?" Daisy asked.

CHAPTER SEVENTEEN

JAMES D. MILLWARD

November 8, 1912 – The Wedding

I told Pearl Wolford that most men in these parts don't go for a long courtship, but ours is probably on record for bein' the shortest courtship in these parts. I went to meet Pearl's family at the end of September and here we are, six weeks later, gettin' married.

Mum was glad that I'd finally found a woman to marry. She said most men are married with several children by the time they're thirty years old. Guess I just never looked for anyone to marry, until I met Pearl.

"I thought ya were too shy to talk to girls. It sure took ya long enough to find one!" my younger brother Ben teased as we were walkin' to the Tarrs Methodist church.

"Yeah, we'd call ya an ol' maid if ya was a girl," Jacob said.

"Now, boys, don't tease your brother," Mum said with a smile.

Funny how Mum still calls us boys; we're all grown men now. I guess to her we'll always be her children, no matter our ages. My sisters were probably already at the church with Pearl and her family. Mum said that I couldn't see my bride before the weddin' or it would cause bad luck. I never heard of such a thing, but I went along with the women's plannin' on my weddin'.

We didn't have many people comin' to the church. My family, Pearl's family, and the Funk family were comin'. I suppose a few of the men I work with in the mine and their families will come. Some of my friends are Catholic so they won't come to our Methodist church but will come to the reception later this afternoon.

I wasn't sure what to expect. I talked with Pearl about the reception but she said the women would take care of all that was needed. If I wanted to serve beer or alcohol that was up to me, but I'm not much of a drinker so we decided to have a dry weddin'. Some of the men at work said that was a crazy idea. They told me that everyone looked forward to a weddin' just to get drunk and have a big party. Pearl and I didn't feel that way. Her family didn't drink either, so we're doin' what we think is best to start out our life together.

Many of the Catholic immigrants who live in coal patch towns have huge celebrations when they marry. Some last for two or three days. Pearl and I talked 'bout it, and we just want a small, private service at church with immediate family and a few friends to share dinner with us. I can't afford to miss work, and Pearl has been busy gettin' our little shack stocked with canned goods and womanly things.

Pearl isn't a frilly type of woman. She said that she doesn't like lace curtains and fancy dishes. She said she'll be happy with the bare necessities to start out with, and then she'll add what we need after the weddin'. The past few days leadin' up to the weddin' I've been busy workin' in the mine and Pearl's been washin' and scrubbin' everything in the house.

"Jim, I don't want to hear ya callin' our home a shack. I've heard ya talkin' to people, and if ya refer to our home as a 'shack,' that's what they'll think we're livin' in. It's a fine little house, and ya should be proud of it, since ya built it yourself," Pearl said.

I must say that she's right. It no longer looks like a shack. Pearl put up plain, yet pretty, white cotton curtains on all of the windows. She put flowered wallpaper in the kitchen, livin' room, and bedroom. She even put wallpaper on the inside walls of the outhouse. We got a new pie cupboard from the company store, and there's a new coal stove I put in when I built the place.

"Hey, James! Did ya hear me?" Ben shouted.

"No, sorry, Ben! I was thinkin' 'bout somethin'," I replied.

"I bet you were thinkin' on your weddin' night!" Ben teased.

I could feel my face gettin' red, and I hoped Mum didn't hear what Ben had just said. I didn't have my pa to talk with 'bout such things, and I would never ask Mum 'bout what a woman expects on her weddin' night. I've heard some men talk 'bout the women at LaLa's Tavern, or the prostitutes from the bigger cities, but I've never wanted to be with that kind of woman.

Fact is, I never thought much before 'bout sleepin' with a woman. Guess I not only lost my childhood to the coal mine, but I work so much that I didn't have time to go chasin' women. After workin' twelve-hour days for six days a week, Sunday is my only day of rest, and that's exactly what I do; rest! I didn't join the local baseball team, or go to the taverns to drink, or go to barn dances. Well, least not until I went to my first barn dance, where I met Pearl.

My thoughts were runnin' through my head so fast that I was gettin' dizzy. When we got to the church, I just stood at the door for a moment and breathed in the crisp, cold November air. Mum put her arm around my waist and her head on my shoulder.

"Ya ready to become a husband, son?" Mum asked.

"Yes, Mum. I hope I can be as good a husband as Pa was to ya," I replied.

"What ya waitin' for? Let's get inside!" Ben said.

As we walked into the church, I looked immediately towards the pulpit to see my bride. The only person standin' there was ol' Pastor Jenkins.

"Mum, Pearl's not here! What should I do?" I asked.

"Go on up to the front of the church. The bride doesn't come in 'til her husband-to-be is standin' with the minister," Mum laughed.

"Oh! I didn't know that," I exclaimed.

Ben and Jacob laughed, and Mum gave them both a mean look as she pointed to the first pew, where my sisters were already seated.

Mrs. McCarty, the church organist, began playin' music and everyone turned around to look towards the back of the church.

First, Pearl's sister Daisy came up the aisle, holdin' a bouquet of dried fall flowers, and then Pearl and her pa came into the church through the side room, where Sunday School was held for the children. It's no wonder I hadn't see her when we first got here—I hadn't thought to look beyond the front of the church.

It seemed to take Daisy a long time to walk up the center aisle of the church. She'd take a step, and then stop, then take another step. She was sort of keepin' time to the music Mrs. McCarty played. Pearl and her pa walked several paces behind Daisy, goin' ever-so slow. I wondered what Pearl was thinkin', 'cause she looked like she was goin' to turn around and run back down the aisle and out the big church doors.

I wasn't sure how to read Pearl's face. She didn't look exceptionally happy, nor did she look sad. She wasn't smilin' or lookin' 'round at anyone but me. Our eyes seemed to lock when she got close enough that I could see her face. I'd never been to a weddin' before, so I wasn't sure of what to do.

"Who gives this woman away?" Pastor Jenkins asked.

"I do!" Pearl's pa replied as he leaned towards me to place Pearl's hand in mine.

The weddin' ceremony went so quickly that I hardly remember what was actually said. When Pastor Jenkins said, "You may kiss your bride," I gave Pearl a quick kiss on the cheek and turned toward the congregation to leave the church as quickly as I could.

"Jim, please slow down!" Pearl whispered as she placed her hand in the crook of my arm.

"Oh, I'm sorry!" I whispered back as I tried to slow my racin' heart.

We walked to the back of the church, where everyone was waitin' to congratulate us. Pearl's mum was cryin' and Daisy was bubblin' over with excitement. Ya would have thought it was Daisy who was getting' married instead of Pearl.

"Stand here beside me to greet the guests as they come out of the church," Pearl said as we stood close to the big, open doors.

Everyone came past us on their way outside, shakin' our hands and kissin' Pearl's cheeks. They all lined the path we'd walk from the church to the road leadin' to Frye Hollow, where Pearl's family would host our weddin' dinner.

Once everyone was out of the church, Pearl and I walked between them all as they commenced throwin' rice at us. I guessed this was another tradition I'd never heard of.

The Funk family had a wagon, lined with straw, to transport everyone to the Wolford homestead. They'd even thought ahead by bringin' quilts for me and Pearl to cover up with. November is the beginnin' of winter in the Laurel Mountains, and the wind was blowin' up an early storm.

The afternoon passed quickly, with much food and laughter. When it began gettin' dark outside, Toby Funk offered to drive me and Pearl to our little house in Snydertown. I helped Pearl up into the wagon and then we snuggled under a woolen quilt. The horses trotted the two miles to our house in record time.

"Thank ya for the ride, Toby!" I said as I helped Pearl get down from the big hay wagon.

"I'm glad to be of service. Congratulations!" Toby shouted, as the team of workhorses stomped their feet in anticipation of goin' home to their barn.

Pearl waved at Toby and then she hurried inside to light the kerosene lamp that was sittin' on the kitchen table. When I entered the kitchen, Pearl stood perfectly still in front of the bedroom door.

"Jim, can ya give me a minute to get ready for ya?" she whispered.

"Take all the time ya need. How will I know when ya be ready for me?" I asked.

"Soon as ya see the lamp go out, ya can come into the bedroom," Pearl said.

I walked out onto the back porch and looked up at the winter sky. There weren't any stars out tonight, but a crescent moon shone through the dark clouds. I quickly said a prayer to God: *"Dear Father in Heaven, please help me to be a good husband."*

I turned back to go into the kitchen when I saw the lantern go dim. As I walked into the bedroom I could hear Pearl breathin' softly. I got into bed and wrapped my new bride in my arms. Suddenly all of the nervousness of the day was gone.

"I love ya, Pearl!" I whispered.

"I love ya too, James," she replied.

I guess I didn't need any instructions on my weddin' night. Pearl and I seemed to be made for each other. I'd never realized that lovin' a woman could be so wonderful, and by the sounds that came from my new bride's lips, she surely must feel the same.

It seemed that we'd only been asleep for a short while when we heard loud noises comin' from our backyard. I knew that I had to go to work in the mornin', but it was much too early for goin' to work.

A raucous bunch of men and young girls were circlin' our house on horseback, makin' lots of noise. They were ringin' cowbells, shootin' guns, and blowin' rams' horns. Some of the women were beatin' on pots and pans and whoopin' it up.

Pearl and I ran out onto the porch to see what was goin' on.

"Hey, big brother! We're serenadin' ya!" Benjamin shouted.

"What ya be doin' that for? It's the middle of the night!" I shouted back.

Pearl wrapped the housecoat tighter around her thin waist and stomped her foot as she shouted, "Ya all just git on back home. Jim has to go to work soon and he needs his sleep."

That only made the group laugh louder and make more noise.

"Let's just go on back inside and ignore them. Maybe they'll go away," I said.

"Mum warned me 'bout the neighbors serenadin' us. She said it's a tradition most farmers like to keep up. Mum said that when my aunt Tillie got married, they pulled her and Uncle Matt right out of their bed and then drove them around the neighborhood on a manure spreader. Ya better lock the door, Jim. I don't want 'em comin' in the house," Pearl said.

Pearl and I blew out the lantern and jumped back into our bed. We snuggled under the covers, tryin' to block out all of the noise comin' from outside by coverin' up our heads. We laughed and tickled each other's ribs like we were children. It wasn't long before the crowd left our place and headed on home. I'm sure all of the men had jobs to go to, so that saved me and Pearl from being carried out into the night.

I never did see who all of those people were that preformed our "serenade" but I am sure that my younger brothers were in on it, as well as my new sister-in-law, Daisy.

CHAPTER EIGHTEEN

PEARL MILLWARD

August 21, 1913 – Motherhood

I can't say that I've ever really wanted to be a mother. When most young girls were actin' silly and droolin' over the boys, I was at home workin' with my mum. I enjoy gardening and keepin' a tidy house, and Mum was glad that I helped her.

I didn't plan on meetin' Jim Millward, let alone on marryin' him, but it all happened so fast. I was on my way to bein' an ol' maid when my sister Daisy talked me into goin' to a barn dance. Jim and I met in September, fell in love, and got married in November.

Now here I am: twenty-five years old with a new babe in my arms. Jim stayed up with me all night, pacin' the floor, and lookin' in on me every few minutes. Mum came yesterday afternoon to help me deliver her first grandchild. Since there is no longer a midwife livin' in the patch ya can get ol' Doc Noon from Youngwood or have another woman help ya to deliver your young'uns.

Jim and I couldn't afford to pay a doctor to come for a house call, so I just prayed that I wouldn't have any complications havin' the baby. I guess God heard my plea, 'cause I delivered a healthy baby girl before sunup this mornin'.

I didn't have any girls' names picked out 'cause I was sure we'd have a boy. I wanted to name him James David, after his pa. I asked Jim if he minded if I named the baby after my grandmother who is still back in England, which was fine with him. So, our little girl is named Ester Ann Millward.

"I don't think I've ever seen such a tiny human bein'!" Jim said as he looked at the baby in my arms.

"Would ya like to hold her?" I asked.

"No! I could break her! I have to get to work now," Jim replied.

"Just hold her for a minute, Jim. Let her hear your voice so she'll know who her pa is," I said.

Jim took Ester from my arms, holdin' her like she was a tiny bird in his big, calloused hands. I watched as he gently kissed the top of her head, and then he put her back in my arms.

"I'll hold her more tonight when I get home from work," Jim said as he hurried from our bedroom.

I heard him say a few words to my mum and then the back door slammed.

"Pearl, ya be feelin' all right?" Mum asked as she walked into my bedroom.

"I'm tired, and a bit hungry," I replied.

"I'll get ya some tea and a nice, thick slice of bread toasted over the coal stove. Ya don't want to eat too much right now, but in a while I'll make ya a big breakfast if ya want," Mum said.

"Mum, how will I know when to feed the baby?" I asked.

"Oh, she'll let ya know when she's hungry. Jim brought ya a surprise in from the barn before he left for work," Mum said.

"I didn't hear him comin' back in the house. What did he bring?" I asked.

Mum didn't answer me, she just turned and went back to the kitchen. I heard her pullin' somethin' across the wooden floor. When she got to the bedroom door she came through it, rear end first, as she pulled something along into the room with her. I couldn't sit up any straighter 'cause I didn't want to disturb the baby, but I could see as Mum got nearer to the bed, the object she was pullin' was very heavy.

When she got close to me, she turned and gave me a full view of my surprise.

"Oh, Mum, it's beautiful!" I cried.

"Yes, it is. Jim made this cradle himself. He kept it hidden in the barn so you wouldn't see it," Mum replied.

"Who made the mattress and the blanket?" I asked.

"Your mother-in-law Anna made the mattress pad and pillow. Daisy crocheted the afghan, and I made the blanket and pillowcase. Do ya like the design that I embroidered on it?" Mum asked.

"It's all perfect. Thank you so much. When do ya think Daisy and Anna will come to see the baby?" I asked.

"I look for Anna to be here any time now, and Daisy will come after she gets the chores done. I was plannin' on makin' a big pot of soup so we'd have food for everyone who comes to visit, and there'll be some for Jim's supper, too," Mum replied.

"Would ya like me to put Ester in the cradle so ya can rest for awhile?" Mum asked.

"I am tired, but I just don't want to stop lookin' at her. She's so beautiful, Mum," I said.

"That she is, but ya need to rest while she's sleepin'. Just call out when she awakens and I'll come back in to get her for ya," Mum said as she put Ester in the cradle.

Mum pulled the cradle next to my bed and I turned on my side to watch my sleepin' baby. Suddenly I realized just how Mum must feel 'bout me and Daisy. Ya never really know how much your mum loves ya until you've had a daughter of your own: lookin' at that tiny face, and her soft downy hair, and knowin' that this child came from me and Jim's love.

God is amazin', I thought as I drifted off to sleep.

I awoke to find Anna sittin' on the rockin' chair, hummin' softly to Ester. I'd never felt very close to Jim's mother, but seein' her face as she looked down at my baby made me realize that she is a loving and carin' woman. She had that same look my own mum had earlier this morning when she'd first laid eyes on Ester.

"Did I wake ya, Pearl?" Anna asked.

"No, I slept enough. Is Ester hungry yet?" I asked.

"Yes, I think she is. She was just beginnin' to fuss, so I picked her up and rocked a bit."

Anna got up from the rockin' chair and handed baby Ester to me. The baby started to cry, and I began to get upset, which made the baby cry even more.

"Anna, would ya ask Mum to come here," I cried.

"Of course, I'll be in the kitchen if ya need me," Anna replied.

As Anna entered the kitchen, my mum, Abigail Wolford, was settin' the table for lunch. Whatever was cookin' on the coal stove sure smelled good.

"Pearl needs ya to come help her with the baby," Anna said.

"Is somethin' wrong?" Abigail asked.

"No, the babe is hungry and Pearl seems a bit overwhelmed as to how to begin feedin' her," Anna replied.

"I was afraid of that. Earlier she asked me how she'd know when the baby was hungry and I could tell she was worried 'bout how to nurse Ester," Abigail said as she turned to go into the bedroom.

Anna went to the stove to stir the soup that was in the big cannin' pot. Abigail had prepared chicken noodle soup and homemade bread. Mum surely had me in mind when she'd decided on the meal. Chicken noodle soup would be the mildest thing on my stomach and would be good for a nursin' baby, too.

"Mum, why is she cryin' so much?" I asked.

"She's just hungry. Don't be upset, dear. Open the front of your nightgown and offer her your breast," Mum said.

I tried to give Ester my breast, but she wouldn't suckle, and then I began to cry, too.

"Pearl, calm down and let her search for your nipple. Once she finds it, she'll suck, but you must stay calm. Ester can sense when you're upset and it makes her upset," Mum said.

I took a deep breath and did as Mum instructed, and Ester rubbed her tiny face all around my breast until she found my nipple. Once she latched on, I had to laugh at how she began to suckle and make little noises. I felt my milk begin to flow down inside my breast to my nipples, and within minutes Ester had milk drippin' from her tiny chin.

"See, that's not so hard," Mum said.

"Mum, I couldn't stand to hear her cry. I didn't know what to do," I said.

"You'll figure it all out. Babies cry when they are hungry, wet, or sick. In no time at all you'll know exactly what Ester wants just by the sound of her cries, and you'll stop bein' upset when she cries. That's her way of tellin' her mum what she needs," Mum said.

It warmed my heart to hear my mum callin' me a mum. I was never the kind of girl who thought much 'bout havin' babies or takin' care of another human bein'. This is goin' to be a challenge for me. Jim won't be able to help with this part of carin' for a young'un, but I sure hope he will help when she begins to walk and talk.

Later on in the day, I heard a knock on the front door. No one ever comes to our front door, as all of our family members and friends enter the kitchen through the back door. I listened to see if I could hear the voice of the person visitin'.

"Pearl, ya have a guest, and she brought ya a baby gift. Do ya feel like visitin'?" Mum asked.

"Who is it?" I asked.

"Her name is Leona Mizerack and she came here from Czechoslovakia five years ago. She and her husband Andrew live across the field," Mum replied.

"Help me to prop up on some pillows, and straighten my hair, and then you may fetch her in," I said.

Mum helped me to make myself presentable, and then she went to the front room to get Leona. As soon as she entered the room I knew we'd be friends. She had the most remarkable face, like that of an angel. She was carrying a wicker basket covered with a crocheted blanket.

"Good day, Mrs. Millward! I'm Leona Mizerack. Please call me Leona," she announced at once.

"Good day! What brings you to visit this day?" I asked.

"I heard that you were expectin' a baby and I made a small blanket for the wee one. I also brought ya a few items that I'd made for my baby," Leona replied.

"That's very kind of ya, but how did ya know that I had my baby today?" I asked.

"Oh, I'm so sorry to intrude. I didn't know your babe was born today, I was just makin' a social call to give ya these things. I can come back another day," Leona said.

"No, don't go. Tell me 'bout yourself, Leona," I said.

"I came to America in 1909 and I had my baby shortly after we arrived here. I didn't know anyone, but a lady named Mary Harris Jones came to visit me. She brought me several baby gifts and a quart of soup. Although Mary was seventy-three years old at the time, we became the best of friends. Oh, how I do miss Mary," Leona said.

"What happened to her?" I asked.

"I guess she just got tired and died of old age, but what a character she was. She came to Westmoreland County to support the United Mine Workers in their strike. A number of the miners' wives had been arrested that summer of 1910 for harassin' strikebreakers and company security personnel. You see, Mary encouraged the women to bring their babies and small children with them when they were sentenced by the court in Greensburg. The presidin' judge sentenced the women to pay a $30 fine or serve 30 days in jail. Well, they were unable to pay so the women were jailed along with their children, for they had no one else to care for them. While the women were bein' processed for imprisonment Mary instructed them to sing the whole night long," Leona said.

"Why did she do a thing like that?" I asked.

"Well, the sheriff's home is next door to the jail, as well as several hotels, lodgin' houses, and other homes. The sound of women singing all through the night kept most of the townspeople awake. Mary brought food and milk to the women and, after five days of sleeplessness, the townspeople angrily demanded that the judge order the women's release. So the incident has become known as 'the women who sang their way out of jail,' and I was one of those women," Leona proudly stated.

"That's a very colorful story, Leona. Where does your husband work now?" I asked.

"He works the coke ovens in several areas. Sometimes he's at the Tarrs ovens, but he goes to Old Bethany and Alverton if they need help. We only had the one baby— Elsa was her name. She died last year of whooping cough," Leona replied.

"I'm sorry to hear that," I replied. Neither of us said anything for a long time, and then Leona walked to the bedroom door.

"I'll come to visit in a week or so when ya are feelin' more like company," Leona whispered.

"Thank you, I'd like that," I said as she quietly left.

I was complete perplexed by this visit. I'd never met nor heard of Leona Mizerack before, but my heart went out to her for the death of her baby, and for the loneliness I sensed within her voice. I'd have to ask Mum if she ever heard the story of "Mother Jones."

MOTHERHOOD

The birth of a woman's first baby is always a special time. Ya learn just what you're made of, for it's no easy task. With each new child, you'd think it would be less stressful, but for me life only got harder. Ester was only three years old when

I had Faith, and then Mary a year after that. Our first son was born in 1920 and Jim was so happy that we had finally gotten a son. We named him James David Millward.

My days are hard. Takin' care of four young'uns and doin' the housework, the gardenin', and the cookin' tires me out. Jim works as much as he could at the mine but sometimes I feel like I'm alone in raisin' the family.

When I became pregnant again in 1923 I swore it would be my last baby. On December 23, 1923 I had a baby girl. We named her Grace. For, by the grace of God, I hope she'll be my last child.

CHAPTER NINETEEN

ANNA MILLWARD

March 1, 1936 –Family Sorrow

When my granddaughter Grace came runnin' into my kitchen, I knew by the sound of her voice that somethin' was mighty wrong. She's my quiet little one, and at thirteen years old she rarely runs anywhere. Sometimes I watch her walkin' to school and she seems as though she's in a world of her own. Guess it must be all of the readin' she does—keeps her mind occupied.

"Grace, what's wrong?" I asked.

Grace ran into my arms and began to sob. I held her close and rubbed her back until she could catch her breath and calm down.

"Grandma, Jimmy is awful sick. Mum called for Doc Noon to come. He's got a really high fever and he's talkin' outta his head. Pa went to work and Mum's furious. She wanted him to stay home today 'cause she said she had a bad omen in her dreams," Grace cried.

"Now, Grace, I don't think that a bad dream means that somethin' bad will happen to Jimmy. He's only sixteen and I'm sure he'll pull out of whatever it is that's givin' him a fever," I replied.

"No, not this time, Grandma. He's had an earache for 'bout a week, and now the fever and a terrible headache. His neck is stiff, too. Mum's not sure, but she heard that meningitis is goin' round," Grace said.

"Oh, dear, that is bad. Maybe we should take time to pray 'bout this. God can heal Jimmy if He wants to," I said.

Grace and I sat across from each other at the kitchen table, and I reached across to hold both of her tiny hands in mine. Grace was shakin' and tears rolled down her pretty face. Her dark brown hair hung in her eyes as she bent her head to pray. The scar on the left side of her face that was caused at birth is barely visible now that she was fillin' out and growin' into a woman.

"Dear Heavenly Father, please be with our child Jimmy and heal him of the fever. Take away his pain and infection. If it be Thy will, restore this child's health. In Jesus name! Amen!"

"Grandma, do ya believe that God will heal Jimmy?" Grace asked.

"I don't know what God's plans are, but it never hurts to talk to Him 'bout what we want. Although, sometimes we just don't get what we want in this life. I begged God to spare your grandfather, to keep him here with me, but God had a need for William in Heaven. I've seen many deaths in Wales and in America. Coal minin' is a hard life, and many have died for various reasons that can't be helped. All we can do is pray and know that we will see our loved ones in Heaven someday," I replied.

"How do ya know we'll see them in Heaven?" Grace asked.

"Because it says so in the Bible and God did not spare His own Son. He let Jesus die so that many will have eternal life. Do ya believe that, Gracie?" I asked.

"I suppose I do, but when it's my brother who's dyin' I'm just not so sure," Grace replied.

"Faith is a hard thing to have. It's one thing to read the Bible and listen to the pastor on Sunday in church, but to put that faith into action is hard to do when we come upon hard times. Now is when we need to stand together and remember God's promises, and reflect on the people we've loved and lost. I pray we'll see them again one day. God willing!" I said. "Come on, I'll walk home with ya. Maybe Doc Noon is there by now."

Grace and I walked through my back yard to the two-story house my son James built. Our yards are connected by a large garden and a maple tree that Pearl planted when she and James were first married. The tree is already big enough to hang a swing made out of rope and an old wooden board. How I love sittin' on my back porch in the evenin' and watchin' the grandchildren play on that swing and climb the branches of that tree. There is a pump with a shiny black iron handle where Pearl gets her water. I have a springhouse, and carried my water in from there until James put in a gravity system for me. With that, the water flows into a holdin' tank made of concrete that's located just a few feet from my back porch.

As soon as we entered the kitchen I went to the stove and put on a fresh pot of coffee. There was a chill in the air, and I figured that the doctor might like a cup of coffee to warm himself after lookin' in on Jimmy. Pearl and I both feel right at home in each other's kitchens. She often comes to visit me after all of the children go to school.

We help each other with bakin'. There are many desserts that we make only on holidays. Christmas is a time for Johnny Bull Puddin' and at Easter we make hot cross buns. Bakin' days are usually at Pearl's house 'cause she needs more of the goodies than I do. With a family of seven, it seems like we're always bakin' bread, and we bake pies every Saturday to have for Sunday dinner after church.

Monday is always wash day and, since I live alone, we have an agreement that I bring my dirty clothes to Pearl's house and she washes them with her things, and then we both hang all of the laundry out on the clothesline. Most of the neighbors have the same routine as we do. News travels throughout the coal patch town by way of the women gossipin' at their clotheslines.

Most everyone in the patch has the same schedule. Ya can always count on Monday bein' homemade vegetable soup day, 'cause on Sunday ya have roast beef and mashed potatoes for dinner. With everyone havin' large families it only makes sense to stretch out the food as much as ya can. The left-over beef from Sunday's meal sure does make tasty soup on Monday. The more children ya have, the more vegetables ya put in the pot. Oh, how good the soup tastes with big, thick slices of homemade bread with lots of butter spread on them.

We don't always have butter. It depends on if the cow is givin' milk—she could go dry for a time between havin' calves. One thing 'bout livin' in the patch: Everyone shares as best they can. If one family has extra milk, they'll trade a gallon jar for a couple dozen eggs. When it's butcherin' time, the family that has a lot of whole-hog sausage trades a few pounds of that for a rump roast, or for a few roastin' chickens.

I was so busy thinkin' on my blessings that I didn't hear Pearl come out of Jimmy's bedroom.

"Anna, would ya like to go in and see Jimmy?" Pearl asked.

"Yes, I would. Is the doctor in there with him?" I asked.

"He is, and he told me to send for Jim at the mine. Oh, Anna, I'm so afraid that Jimmy won't make it," Pearl cried.

170

I went to Pearl and put my arms around her. I could feel her shakin' as she sobbed into my shoulder. I held back my tears, wantin' to be strong for her and for Gracie.

"I'll come right out, Pearl. Pour yourself a cup of coffee. I just made a fresh pot," I said.

I gently opened the bedroom door and walked to the side of the bed. Doctor Noon was sittin' on a chair beside Jimmy's bed. His head was in his hands, and I wasn't sure if he was prayin' or just tired, so I didn't say anythin' until he looked up at me.

"Oh, Anna, I'm glad to see ya here. Not much else I can do for the boy. We may have to quarantine the house and the family for awhile. Jimmy has spinal meningitis as near as I can tell," Doctor Noon said.

"How did he get it?" I asked.

"Some people from Scottdale came down with it 'bout a month ago. I heard from Doc Gilbert that he was treatin' some of the railroad men. Could be they carried it to the other towns with the freight they delivered. 'Course they would have had to cough or sneeze on people to spread it. I have to watch closely to see if anyone else comes down with a high fever. Jimmy is just too far gone. He's already got the stiff neck and partial paralysis, and he has mastoids behind his ears. No amount of medicine will stop the spread of it in his body now," the doctor replied.

"Pearl said ya asked that James come home from work early. Do ya think Jimmy will go that quickly?" I cried.

"Yes, Anna, I don't think it'll be long now. Even if Pearl had called me a few days ago, this infection is a bad one. We just don't know enough 'bout it yet to know what drugs to treat it with effectively," Doc said.

I put my hand on my grandson's cheek, and he felt like he was burnin' up. Doctor Noon had a pan of cool water on the stand beside the bed, so I reached for the rag to bathe Jimmy's face. He didn't move, or say anythin', and then I heard a faint groan escape his cracked, dry lips.

"It's all right, Jimmy boy. Grandmum is here with ya," I whispered.

There was no response to my voice but I still kept wipin' his face and neck with the cool water. I heard that sometimes just havin' someone ya love nearby can bring a person back, and give them the strength to want to get well. I silently prayed as I kept wipin' his face.

"Anna, would ya fetch Pearl in, please?" Doc asked.

"Yes, of course," I replied as I got up immediately to go out of the room.

I turned to look at Jimmy before I went out the door, and the doctor was listenin' to his heart with a stethoscope. He looked up at me and shook his head. I knew at once. My grandson was dead.

"Pearl, where is Gracie?" I asked.

"She went to fetch her pa," Pearl replied.

"The doctor wants ya to come in at once," I said.

Pearl ran to the bedroom and I walked in behind her. Since James wasn't home from work yet, I wanted to be with Pearl, so she wouldn't have to face this alone. When she looked at Doctor Noon, and then down at her son, Pearl began to wail and cry. She ran to the bed and laid her head on Jimmy's chest. I went to stand beside her, as my own tears could not be stopped.

It wasn't long before James and Gracie came through the back door. They must have run all the way from the mine because neither of them could speak. Gracie began to cry.

"Grandma, is Jimmy dead?" Gracie asked, for she could hear her mother's sorrowful cries.

"Yes, Gracie, he just passed a few minutes ago," I whispered.

James was already in the bedroom as Gracie and I were talkin', and then he began to cry. Doctor Noon came out of the bedroom, and gently closed the door so that the parents could be alone with their dead child. I'm sure this is a part of his job that he'll never get used to.

"Doctor, would ya like a cup of coffee?" I asked.

"Yes, thank ya, Anna. I'll stay awhile until James and Pearl are ready to discuss funeral arrangements," Doctor Noon replied.

"Can I go in, Grandma?" Gracie asked.

"Oh, Gracie, yes, of course. Go be with your parents," Doctor Noon said, before I could answer her.

I went to the cupboard, gettin' cups, saucers, and the sugar bowl out, and then to the icebox for some cream for the coffee. Just yesterday Pearl had made Jimmy's favorite cookies, pumpkin spice with raisins, in the hopes that he would be well enough to eat one. She was kind enough to send me down a half-dozen for my snack last night. I looked in the pie cupboard and found the tin that she kept cookies in, then put several on a plate.

Although I didn't feel like eatin' anythin', I wanted to offer somethin' to the good doctor.

"Thank ya, Anna. These cookies sure do look good," he said.

"They're the best. Pearl must have brought the recipe from England. My aunt Ester made these same cookies when I was a girl, and they taste much the same," I replied.

We sat in silence for a long while, until finally James, Pearl, and Gracie came out of the bedroom.

"Doctor Noon, what do we do now?" James asked.

"First, I have to prepare the body for burial, and then I'll have to quarantine ya all for two weeks. Ya do realize that ya can't have a wake here?" Doctor Noon asked.

"That's just not right!" Pearl cried.

"Now, Pearl, it can't be helped. We don't want to spread the disease. I'll send word to Pastor Jenkins and see if he can come to the house to do a funeral service for just us family," James replied.

We had Jimmy's funeral the very next mornin'. Doctor Noon prepared his body right there in his bed, and James made his coffin from new pine boards he got from the company store. The only ones who could come to the funeral were Pearl, James, Gracie, Pastor Jenkins, Doctor Noon, and me. None of my other grandchildren could come to pay their respects to their little brother.

After the funeral, James took all of the bedding from Jimmy's bed outside to burn, and Gracie sat in the kitchen with me. Pearl went upstairs to her bedroom, yet we could still hear her sobs. I prepared a meal for the four of us, but no one had much of an appetite.

"Mum, I don't know how we'll make it if I can't go to work for two weeks," James said as he came into the kitchen and sat down across from me at the table.

"Ya can't be worryin' 'bout that now. I'll give ya what I have in my cookie jar, and we'll have plenty of food. Doctor

Noon said that I'll be quarantined, too, but I can still come to help you and Pearl," I replied.

"Mum, I can't be takin' money from ya," James said.

"James, go upstairs to your wife. She needs ya near at a time like this. I'm gonna go on home after I put all this food away. Seems like there's nothin' more I can do," I said.

James went upstairs, and Gracie said she also wanted to be alone, so I tidied up the kitchen and walked down through the back yard to my own little house. I was no sooner in the door than my head started spinnin' and I felt weak. I told myself that I was probably just over-tired and stressed from the last two days.

I went to bed at once and I must have slept for twenty-four hours, because when I awoke James was standin' over me, shoutin' my name.

"James, what ya be shoutin' for?" I asked.

"Mum, we didn't see ya outside all evenin', so I just come to check on ya and ya be burnin' up. Ya didn't hear me comin' in or callin' ya name. Are ya sick?" James asked.

"I feel real bad. It came on me quick, soon as I got home yesterday I felt dizzy. Maybe ya should call Doc Noon," I said.

"I'll have to ask Gracie to go to Mary's house. She lives the closest, and bein' that she's family no one will get excited that we've broken the quarantine. I'll come right back, Mum. Just stay in bed," James replied.

James didn't have to tell me to stay in bed, for I couldn't have gotten up if I'd wanted to. I can't remember ever bein' so sick. I slept off and on all night. I don't remember talkin' with Doc Noon, but James told me that he'd been here and would come back with some medicine in a few hours.

"Mum, can ya wake up for me, please?" James cried.

"Oh, James, are ya still here?" I said.

"Yes, I've been here all along. Doctor Noon says ya have what Jimmy had, and ya be real sick. Mum, I love ya. I'm prayin' ya get well," James whispered.

"James, I love ya too. Don't be a-frettin' over me. I'll be fine. I want ya to take my cookie jar home with ya. I don't have much, but I trust ya to divide my belongings with all my children. Tell Benjamin, Sarah, Jacob, Delilah, and Elizabeth that I love them all dearly. Have ya sent word to them 'bout Jimmy?" I asked.

"Mum, don't talk like this. Ya can't die. I need ya, Mum," James cried.

I heard someone comin' into my bedroom, and then I saw Doctor Noon, Gracie, and Pearl all standin' beside my bed. James got down on his knees and was holdin' my hand. I couldn't hear what anyone was sayin', and then I saw a bright light. I heard William callin' out my name.

Oh, how sweet the sound! My beloved, my husband. Together again!

CHAPTER TWENTY

JAMES D. MILLWARD

January 1, 1940 – Jobs Lost and Gained

This is the first day of 1940, and I can't find any reason to celebrate. Last night people throughout all the coal patch towns were havin' a high ol' time—drinkin', shootin' guns, and bangin' pots and pans to ring in the new year. I sure don't know where this tradition comes from but I, for one, could do without it.

There just isn't much to be happy 'bout in my house anymore. Since Jimmy died four years ago Pearl has turned into a very different person. Gone is the sweet girl I married. Now she is always in a bad mood and mean as a bear. She was so mad that I had to work all night on New Year's Eve that she hasn't spoken to me for three days.

When the Bortz Coal Company of Uniontown purchased the mine back in 1932 there were a lot of changes made. Bortz Coal Company bought the mine but not the town of Central—many people had to leave and find other homes to live in. The company also stopped coal production, to do repairs and to install new railroad tracks.

For the past eight years my job at the mine hasn't been stable so, with money being hard to come by, I've taken several part-time jobs. There's a tavern just down the road from our house called Snydertown Tavern. I work as a bartender every night, including last night, and I couldn't get the people to leave the tavern. I finally had to turn out the lights and chase them out the door.

"Jim, wait up," Joe Imbellisario called as he came running down the hill from Rocktown.

"What ya be doin' out so early on this New Year's Day?" I asked.

"I just needed to take a bit of a walk. Ginny's mad 'bout my drinkin' too much last night," Joe replied.

"Well, does she have reason to be mad? Did ya go and do somethin' foolish?" I asked.

"Awe, Jim ya know how it is at LaLa's Tavern. After ya have a few pints, those women of the evenin' bribe ya to get free drinks. I'd never be with any of them, ya know, but I did spend too much money, and when I got home Ginny was ready to kill me. She beat me over the head with a broom, and let me pass out on the back porch. I just woke up and figured I'd go with you to tend the fire at Snydertown Tavern," Joe replied.

"Ya be welcome to help me tend the fire, but I'll not be servin' ya drink. The tavern is closed today, but I have to keep the fire goin' so nothin' freezes. I bet ya sure got cold passed out on the porch," I said.

"I think my toes are frostbit. I can hardly feel 'em," Joe said.

I had to laugh at Joe, and his Italian accent made his story even funnier. I've heard how the women from Italy have ferocious tempers. I also know they are some of the best cooks in the patch. The Imbellisario family, large with many children, came to America seekin' work in the mine. Many times Joe's offered me a slice of homemade bread, or a pie made of bread dough, cheese, tomato sauce, and hot pepperoni. This pie folds in half, makin' it easy for him to carry in his lunch pail. He calls it "pizza" and says it's an old recipe from his great-grandmother back in Sicily. It sure does taste good. Joe says it's best right out of the oven, bubblin' hot, but in the mine we have to eat it cold.

"How's ya wife doin' Jim?" Joe asked.

"Oh, she's 'bout like your wife this mornin', Joe. Madder than a hornet that I worked all night at the tavern. I don't know why she's mad 'cause we never celebrate New Year's Eve. Neither of us drinks, and Pearl doesn't talk to the girls all that much. Gracie still lives at home with us, but the others mostly stay away," I said.

"Why is that, Jim?" Joe asked.

"Don't quite know, but Pearl doesn't get on kindly with anyone anymore. Ester went off long ago to marry a man named Gettemy. She lives over in Old Bethany. She's so much like Pearl that they fight every time they do see each other, which isn't very often. Mary ran off with a stranger on a motorcycle. Last we heard, she's livin' in Ohio somewhere," I said.

"Why'd she go and so a fool thing like that?" Joe asked.

"Pearl and Mary got into an awful fight one day over pumpin' water to wash clothes. While Mary was leanin' over to pick up the bucket of water that Pearl had just pumped, Pearl started to pump more water, and then the pump handle hit Mary on her right temple and knocked her clean out. When she came to, she was completely blind. We took her to Mount Pleasant, to a doctor who said she had severe eye damage. He gave her thick eyeglasses and medicine to put in her eyes every day, but she never could forgive her mother. Ya know, Joe, I often thought that Pearl was beatin' on Mary when she was a small child, but it wasn't until after she ran away that Gracie told me just how much Pearl hated Mary. I tried to talk to Pearl 'bout it but she only got mad at Gracie and took a switch to her once I'd gone to work," I explained.

"I'm sorry to hear this, Jim. Don't know what I'd do if my Ginny started beatin' on our young'uns. She has her mother's temper, but she sure does love the children. I've never seen her raise a hand to 'em, but they be so afraid of her yellin' they never do anythin' to get a whippin'," Joe said.

"The sorrowful thin' is, Mary didn't do nothin' to deserve bein' beat, either. Pearl just turned mean over the years. What I didn't see when the girls were younger, I'm seein' now that Jimmy's dead. She's angry all the time," I said.

Joe and I never have such personal conversations when we work in the mine together. I respect him for bein' a reliable worker. I don't think I know of any time that Joe hasn't been at work since he's moved to Rocktown. He's one of the strongest men I've ever seen and he's been called a 'gentle giant' by some of the miners.

"Jim, I heard ya be trainin' young Slim Dugan to set charges in the mine," Joe said.

"Yea, he's one of the fastest learners I've ever seen. Ya know, he can set the charge and be out of harm's way faster than any man I know. My pa taught me to set charges, and I thought pa was good, until I hired Slim. He's accurate with the depth of the drillin' and with timin' his length of fuse. He's been a real asset to our mine. I'm startin' to feel my age, so I'm glad to have a young man to do the dangerous work. Since my knees have been achin' so much, I'm not as fast as I once was," I replied.

<u>Slim Dugan setting dynamite charge in the mine.</u>

When we got to the tavern, Joe and I went in and locked the door behind us. I didn't think there were any sober men left in Syndertown who would come knockin' at the door, but I kept the shade drawn just in case. We went to the basement where the big coal furnace sat. I shook the cinders from the coal furnace and banked the fire with several small buckets of coal, and then Joe and I went up to the bar and sat on the old wooden bar stools.

"Would ya like a bottle of pop, Joe?" I asked.

"Ya have any grape Nehi?" Joe asked.

"I sure do, and I'll join ya by havin' the same," I laughed.

Joe and me sat and talked for 'bout an hour, and then we both figured it was time to git on home and face the music, for we knew our wives weren't gonna be happy with us.

"See ya tomorrow, Joe," I said as we parted ways at my house. Joe still had to walk up to Rocktown Road to his house.

"Thank ya, Jim," Joe replied.

"What ya be thankin' me for, Joe?" I asked.

"For bein' a friend is all," he said.

I stood and watched as Joe climbed the small hill just past our back yard, and I wondered if Ginny would be in a better mood now. Can't say as I blame her for bein' upset. They still have young children, and I'm sure money is tight for them just like it is for every miner. Although Joe shouldn't have wasted it on drink, I see both sides of this argument. Sometimes a man just needs to let off steam and get away from the problems of bein' a coal miner. The danger alone can make ya feel like your life could pass away in an instant. Still, I see how the women feel, too. Their job is never done. Ya just can't walk away from bein' a mother. The children, housework, cookin', and carin' for a husband is a never-endin' job with few rewards other than the love ya can offer each other.

CHAPTER TWENTY-ONE

JAMES D. MILLWARD

December 17, 1944 – Moving On

"Pap, ya have to come home. Somethin's wrong with Mum," Grace cried as she ran into the tavern.

"What seems to be ailin' her, Gracie?" I asked.

"She can't breathe, and she says her arm and shoulder are hurtin' somethin' awful. She looks funny, too. Her face is sort of gray. Can ya come home now, Pap?" Grace asked.

"Ben, can ya tend the bar for me 'til I go and check on Pearl?" I asked my brother who had stopped in for a pint after his shift at the coke ovens.

"Ya go on home, Jim, and I'll stay here 'til I hear from ya on how Pearl's feelin'," Ben replied.

Grace and I swiftly walked the quarter-mile to our house. I knew that Pearl must be in bad shape to have even let Grace come for me. In all the years we've been married, Pearl's never one to baby herself. She's a strong and independent woman.

"Grace, did ya talk with Faith this morning?" I asked as we neared the house.

"No, Mum said she didn't want me to tell Faith she was feelin' poorly 'cause then Faith would come with all of her children, and Mum didn't feel like puttin' up with them all today," Grace replied.

"Well, ya should go up and tell Faith to come down to our house, and then you can watch her young'uns for a bit," I said.

"But, Pap, I don't want to watch Faith's brood, I want to be with Mum," Grace cried.

"Well, how 'bout ya come in with me to check on your mum, and then ya can fetch Faith?" I asked.

"All right, I'll agree to do that, but I'll not be watchin' her kids all day. Borya and Fadeyka fight with Nadia and Doroteya, and if they aren't a-fightin' they're causin' trouble with the neighbor's children. Must be 'cause Faith had to go and marry Dimochka, that ol' Russian from Wynno. He even made her give the children Russian names, and ya can't hardly pronounce 'em. Faith's children are just rotten!" Grace replied.

"Now, Gracie, don't be talkin' 'bout your sister's children like that. Ya never know how your own will turn out, and ya don't know who you'll be fallin' in love with. Maybe ya will end up with a Polish or Italian man," I said.

"Well, I hope that when I have children that I'll make 'em listen, and I don't plan on doin' no courtin' with anyone who isn't Welsh," Grace replied.

I laughed at Grace, and then we went into the house. We stopped talkin' 'bout Faith and her family and we both hurried into the bedroom where Pearl was restin' in her bed. I knew she must be feelin' real bad if she'd go to bed before it got dark outside.

"What ya be doin' home already, Jim?" Pearl asked.

"Gracie came to fetch me, she said ya be feelin' sick," I replied.

"I'm havin' a hard time breathin' and my shoulder is hurtin' so much I can't lift my arm. May just be indigestion," Pearl said.

I sat down on the side of the bed and felt Pearl's head to see if she had a fever, but she felt cold and clammy. I wasn't sure of what to do for her, but I figured I best send for ol' Doc Noon.

"Grace, go tell Borya to run to the mine and have my boss use the telephone to contact Doctor Noon, and then ya can send Faith down to see her mum while ya watch her children," I said.

Grace left at once, without givin' me an argument. As soon as she was out the door I asked Pearl to be honest with me and tell me just what she thought was the matter with her.

"Jim, I'm afraid! I've never had such pain, and I can't think straight. Would ya get me a glass of water?" Pearl asked.

I went outside to the spring to fetch Pearl a glass of fresh, cool water. When I returned to the bedroom Pearl's hands were on her chest and she wasn't breathin'. I screamed her name and tried to shake her awake, but she didn't make a sound. I laid my head on her chest and grasped both of her hands in mine, and then I broke down and cried.

None of us ever know when the good Lord will take us home, but we're never really ready for that day. When the one we love is taken suddenly, it is such a shock that ya don't know which way to turn.

"Pearl, I'm not ready for ya to go to Heaven. What will I do without ya? God, why did ya take my wife?" I sobbed.

By the time Faith came into the bedroom, I was so sick with sorrow that I couldn't comprehend what to do. Grace is our youngest, and our most emotional, child. Even though she's twenty years old I knew she'd just fall apart at findin' her mum dead. Faith's more level-headed and most apt to handlin' the preparations for a wake, but I needed Ester to come home. Ester's the oldest of our children and the most level-headed.

"Pap, what's wrong?" Faith cried as she ran to my side and put her arms around my shoulders.

"Mum's gone, Faith. She's dead!" I whispered.

"Oh, no! She can't be dead. I was just here yesterday to help with the laundry. She was fine, just a bit tired. Pap, what happened to her?" Faith asked.

"I don't know, but Doc Noon might be able to figure out why she died," I replied.

"I'd better go fetch Grace, and I'll have one of the children go for Ester and Mary," Faith said.

When Doc Noon finally got to our house, all of my children were standin' 'round the bed, cryin'. Grace was kneelin' beside the bed with her head on her mum's chest, much like I'd done just a short while ago.

"Sorry it took me so long to get here, Jim. Would the rest of ya please step out of the bedroom so I can talk to your pa?" Doc Noon said.

Once all of the children had gone into the kitchen and closed the bedroom door, Doc Noon went to the bedside and placed his stethoscope on Pearl's chest.

"Doc, she's already dead," I cried.

"I still need to check her, to be sure. Tell me what happened, Jim," Doc Noon asked.

186

"I was at the tavern workin' and Gracie came to get me. She said Pearl had pain in her arm and shoulder and couldn't breathe very well. When I got home she was cold and clammy and holdin' her chest. She asked me for a drink of water, and when I came back with it she was dead," I explained.

"Most likely it was her heart. All of the symptoms point to a heart attack and, given Pearl's age and the number of babies she's had, I'm sure that is what killed her. Do ya want me to call the undertaker for ya, Jim?" Doc Noon asked.

"Yes, but we'll have her body right here at home. She'd want to be laid out in the livin' room, not in a funeral home," I replied.

The next three days passed in a blur. I don't remember who came to view my wife's body, or who brought food, or, for that matter, what was even said to me. I tried my best to console the children and grandchildren, but I couldn't even find any consolation myself. I know that the pastor talked and prayed with me, but I don't remember a word he said. When we buried Pearl in the Tarrs cemetery, I walked home alone while the rest of the family rode in a farmer's wagon.

Once all of our friends and neighbors left, the children and I gathered 'round the kitchen table. I really just wanted to be alone, but I knew that the children needed to talk. I guess it's the same for everyone. Once a loved one dies, ya sit and talk 'bout their life and how much they meant to ya.

"I'm sure glad Mum suggested that my family and me move into the big house and that you and her and Gracie took the small one a few years ago. Mum was always thinkin' 'bout everyone else. She didn't worry 'bout herself," Faith said.

"Yes, Mum was like that. She'd do without just so her family could have more," Ester replied.

"Well, I seen a different side to Mum than the rest of ya saw, but I still loved her," Mary added as she wiped her eyes.

"Mum never got over Jimmy dyin', but maybe now she'll be in Heaven with 'im," Grace whispered.

As I listened to each of my children talk 'bout Pearl, I wanted to feel that I was blessed to have had thirty-two years with her, but it just wasn't enough. Who would take care of the daily chores? Who would make the Johnny Bull Puddin' at Christmas? Who could ever love this ol' man like my Pearl did?

I got up and went outside to sit alongside the house, where Pearl and I used to sit in the cool of the evenin' and talk 'bout our day. I could almost feel her touch my big, rough hand with her chubby little red one. Pearl's hands were always red from doin' the laundry and scrubbin' the floors. She had the hands of a workin' woman, and I'd never had the money or the time to pamper her. One thing is for sure: Pearl Wolford Millward loved me and I love her.

NOTES FROM THE AUTHOR

Life in a coal patch town was the same all over Pennsylvania, West Virginia, and Ohio. It was a harsh, cruel life, full of hardships, death, and sorrow. Although this was true for my family, I can still see the blessings that God has bestowed on me. I never got to meet my grandmum, Pearl Millward, but my pap, James David Millward, was an awesome man who has inspired me just by being the man that he was: a coal miner.

The history of Tarrs, Rocktown, Snydertown, and the Central coal mine was kept alive by my grandfather. For many years his nameplate hung on the outside wall of our little house, which is situated between Rocktown and Snydertown. The nameplate reads *J.D. MILLWARD* and it hung to the right of the front door so that all who entered would know who established this homestead. Grandpap Millward built the house and lived in it until he died on October 29, 1964 at the age of eighty-two. I was eleven years old at the time. I now keep his hard hat, mine lamp, and his nameplate on a shelf in my own house.

My first novel, From *Across the Pond*, and this, my second novel, have been such joys to write. I've researched the history of our area online, in libraries, and in museums. I've talked with many people who knew and/or worked with my grandfather and my mother. My husband, Tom Goodlin, took me to the Tour-Ed Mine and Museum in Tarentum, Pennsylvania so that I could see and feel what it was like to work miles beneath the earth.

My father-in-law, Clyde Goodlin, also taught me many valuable details about his life in the mines as a master mechanic and the chief electrician for Delmont Fuel in

Ruffsdale, Pennsylvania. He, too, had gone into the mines to work at the young age of approximately thirteen. His was another "childhood lost." Before his death, I spent many days talking with him and learning about a time in history that should never be forgotten.

I hope all who read this book will learn from it, be inspired by it, and will share it with your friends and families. Take time to talk with your grandparents, for all too soon the past is gone and we have only our memories.

May God bless you!

Linda A. Goodlin

This is the name plate that was on the house
my grandfather built, where I grew up.

The cap, lantern, and fuel can were used
by my grandfather in the mine.

JOHNNY BULL PUDDING

Pearl Wolford Millward brought with her "from across the pond" this recipe for Johnny Bull Pudding. My mother, Grace Marie Millward Wilkins, made this for our family every year at Christmas time, and I'm sure she had fond memories of her mother as we sat 'round the kitchen table eating it.

1 apple, chopped	2 pkgs. candied pineapple
2 cups sugar	5 teaspoons baking powder
4 eggs	1 teaspoons cinnamon
1 ½ cups ground suet	1 teaspoon allspice
1 teaspoon salt	1 teaspoon nutmeg
1 ½ cups milk	1 cup chopped nuts
2 pkgs. candied cherries (1red, 1 green)	1 cup raisins

Mix all ingredients very well, and then add enough flour to make the mixture very stiff. Form into a firm ball. You may want to separate into two balls, to keep your Johnny Bull Pudding from splitting.

Have a large kettle of water boiling.

Place Johnny Bull Pudding in a clean, white bag—leave a few inches of space above the pudding to allow for rising—and tie top shut. Cheesecloth is too flimsy for this boiled recipe. (*Mum used to use a new white pillowcase or flour sack that she'd washed before making the pudding.*)

Place the bag of pudding into the boiling water and simmer for 3 hours.

Remove the pudding from the bag and roll in sugar and cinnamon. Put in hot oven (375 degrees) for 15 minutes.

This recipe is almost like a fruit cake, only heavier. It does not call for a sauce. However, I've used the sauce recipe with it and it is wonderful.

SAUCE FOR PUDDING

Put into small sauce pan:

2 cups water   ½ cup sugar

2 Tablespoons cornstarch   1 teaspoon vanilla

Bring to a boil, stirring constantly. Once thickened, pour several tablespoons over slices of Johnny Bull Pudding.

RAISIN FILLED COOKIES

(Recipe from Millward Family)

Filling:

2 cups chopped raisins

⅔ cup sugar

1 tablespoon butter

⅔ cup water

Instructions

In a pan over medium heat, cook raisins, sugar, and ⅔ cup of water for 10 to 15 minutes, or until thick, stirring occasionally.

Remove from heat and stir in the butter. Let cool while preparing dough.

Dough:

1 cup sugar   3 teaspoons baking powder

1 cup (2 sticks) butter   1/4 teaspoon salt

1 egg, beaten   1/3 cup milk

3 cups sifted all-purpose flour   2 teaspoons vanilla extract

Instructions

Preheat oven to 350 degrees.

In a bowl, cream sugar and butter together, until fluffy. Add egg and mix well.

In a separate bowl, combine flour, baking powder, and salt, and alternately add milk and vanilla to sugar mixture.

Roll out the dough to ⅛-inch thickness and cut into rounds with a biscuit cutter. Place a teaspoonful of filling in the center of a round, then cover with another round and press edges together.

Bake for 10 to 15 minutes or until golden brown.

PIZZELLES: Italian Anise Cookies

(Old Italian recipe from Anna Goodlin)

12 eggs – beaten   2 Tablespoons vanilla

1 ½ cups vegetable oil   1 large jar Anise Seeds

2 ¼ cup sugar   Flour – approximately
                                 3 cups.

Beat all together until well mixed. Add flour, 1 cup at a time, until batter is stiff—a bit thicker than pancake batter.

Heat the pizzelle iron on both sides over stove burners until hot, brush the iron the first time with vegetable oil. You do not need to brush with oil after each pizzelle.

Bake on each side until lightly browned.

In today's kitchens, electric pizzelle makers, instead of cast-iron ones, are the norm. Follow the manufacturer's directions for baking your pizzelles. This is an old Italian recipe that I got from my mother-in-law. I used her cast-iron pizzelle maker for years until I got a ceramic-top stove. I now use an electric pizzelle maker, but they do not taste quite the same as baking them over a coal or gas stove.

Made in the USA
Monee, IL
07 July 2026